I0477700

Tales of Womanhood Vol 2

Compiled by Maureen Mbondiah-Mandipaza

Tales of Womanhood Vol 2

Tales of Womanhood Volume 2
A Compilation of Inspirational Stories From Women Around The World

© 2019 Tales Of Womanhood and the authors of each story ;- Brenda Dempsey, Hadassah Esther, Heidi Maja, Memory Mbondiah, Michelle Nwosu, Rachel Tracey, Tara Burgin, Tistsi Chipendo

British Library Cataloguing in Publication Data. A catalogue record for this book is available from the British Library.

Published in the United Kingdom by Tales Of Womanhood.
www.talesofwomanhood.org

Paperback: ISBN: 9781798865491

First Edition: March 2019

Categories; Business & Economics – Personal Success
Religion, Christian Life – Inspirational

DEDICATION

A massive congratulations for Vol 2 of the book series Tales of Womanhood. What an amazing journey it has been with so much inspiration to women across the Globe from women just like me and you.

I have come to realise that the difference between us in terms of colour, geographical location, status quo, creed or religion do not remove us from the challenges of Womanhood that affect each one of us across the Globe every day. This truth will only suffice when you take time to examine the tales told by women from different backgrounds and discover how they navigate to a place of restoration healing or even deliverance.

With this in mind I dedicate this book to every woman whatever background, who has been in that place of Womanhood when you have felt like giving up or throwing in the towel. Indeed, some have completely lost hope in the midst of all the challenges that life throws at our lives. This book has been simply designed to encourage you with inspirational real- life stories of women just like me and you who have also passed through your current position but have surpassed and made it to the finish line.

My desire is to see you be inspired to be more and to do more, hence the decision to continue with the book series.

I realise you may not yet have had the opportunity to read the first volume of the Tales of Womanhood Books, but l am happy you are reading this next volume of stories that will change your perspective of life and its challenges.

Remember that every day is step towards your finish line, so it's important to be a work in progress. Time waits for no one therefore it is so important to treat time as an irreplaceable commodity every day because once spent it can never be retrieved. Every day is a work in progress and I encourage you to as the scripture says, 'Let us not become weary in doing good, for at the proper time, we will reap a harvest if we do not give up!' (Galatians 6:9)

There is an emphasis on NOT giving up on your journey or even your challenges. Many women fail because they fail to master the art of never giving up on their purpose.

Sometimes it may seem like the easy way out is to give up, faint, throw in the towel, in all you are going through. Fainting normally happens when someone is running a race, as they get weary, so here we are told that in due season we shall reap, but the condition is not to faint.

I know that when life throws lemons at you it's easier said than done to make lemonade out of it.

As you will see from the women in this book, challenges came, but these did not stop them from aiming for life's best, made lemonade. I can safely say that despite the circumstance's life threw at these women, sheer determination and courage saw them through the worst challenges in life.

One would say they ran a 'good race,' to bring out the best, even in their darkest hour.

I therefore dedicate this book to all, past, present and future contributing authors to the book series of Tales of Womanhood Books and to everyone around the world who takes time to read this book. I encourage you to learn and apply the lessons given to you from these women who have passed through deep waters.

Tales of Womanhood Vol 2

Tales of Womanhood Vol 2

ACKNOWLEDGMENTS

l would like to thank the Almighty God who has been with me from the day this vision was incepted in me. Indeed the storm came after Vol 1 was launched, but giving up was not an option.

Disappointment, discouragement and betrayal all played a part but sheer determination courage and the ability to see past the mud allowed me to gather strength to continue with Vol 2 of the book .

I am eternally grateful for my family, friends and associates who inspire me to continue pushing against all odds.

My family come as my main source of strength to my every accomplishment and my husband Don who l don't seize to praise for allowing me to fly higher as l pursue my vision.

Many women are in place of discouragement because of their choice of partner or spouse. Many continue to suffer abuse on a daily basis at the hands of their spouse or partner.

My prayer is for every woman to be with a man who truly loves and wants the best for them at all times. Women are like flowers that need water to flourish. Women we need love and support to flourish.

I am truly blessed to have a husband who wants me to excel in life as l pursue my purpose so l am truly grateful to God!

I thank my children who put up with my busy crazy schedule. My children Donell, Sean and princess Hannah-Mae, l love you all.

You continue to be my strength and motivators so for this l am eternally grateful.

To my dad Mr Petros Mafikeni-Mbondiah l am grateful for all the teachings and lectures. I can assure you these have become my point of reference- cheers dad!

To my late mother Catherine, May Your Soul Rest In Peace. I know you are smiling from heaven...

I acknowledge every woman who contributed to this amazing piece Rachel, Tsitsi, Tara, Hadassah Esther, Michelle, Hon MP Memory, Heidi, Brenda, Zoe, and of course Susan Brookes-Morris the editor! Without you all, this book would remain only a thought and not a reality! Thank you for sharing your stories with the world, to inspire, influence and ignite dreams and courage.

To you the reader, l hope with the knowledge that your current situation is not your final destination, you will be inspired to rise up against all odds.

To any woman who is on the verge of breakdown l want you to hold up, don't throw in the towel today, remember many women just like you have walked that same path, climbed that same mountain, crossed that very road, even swam through that same river and have come out stronger and even more successful than ever. There is always light at the end of the tunnel and today l and many of these women in Tales of Womanhood want to inspire you to await that light.

Enjoy the read

Regards
Mo

Tales of Womanhood Vol 2

Tales of Womanhood Vol 2

Tales of Womanhood Vol 2

CONTENTS

Tales of Womanhood Vol 2

ZOE BENNETT

Zoe Bennett has a unique true life story which she titles "Through Adversity Breeds Success". This includes childhood abuse, rape and persevering through seven trial postponements and death threats following the murder of her father

She uses these tragic incidents to reinforce that when life overwhelms you and you cannot see a way of succeeding, you can still find the inner motivation, strength, strategy and drive to ensure you are successful if you utilise your mindset.

Even though she has gone through so much adversity, she continues to help others through theirs. She helps by talking at and providing workshops in schools, charitable organisations, the public sector and corporate industry, where she talks about her background and how despite not succeeding in school, she went on to turn it around and obtain a Masters in Tourism management, now runs a thriving training company Training Personified and has written a book about networking called Networking Personified.

Zoe helps many different communities and is diverse and inclusive in her approach. She helps those who have faced domestic violence, the youth, the unemployed cancer victims, mental health sufferers, the disabled and many others.

Zoe is also the founder of the black tie (MBCC) Midlands Business and Community Charity Awards , an NSPCC Birmingham Business Board Member and Member of the Fairness in Policing Critical Reference Groups for West Midlands Police.

Her other achievements include:-
- NatWest Finalist "Entrepreneur For Good" West Midlands 2017
- Enterprise Vision Awards Finalist – Training and Coaching 2017
- Awarded In New Delhi, India at WEF "Iconic Woman Creating a Better World For Others" May 2017
- Awarded June 2017 at Powerhouse Global for "Inspirational Woman of the Year"
- Awarded Outstanding Diva at the Divas of Colour Awards 2017
- Awarded Human Excellency Award from United Nations Mission of International Relations 2016
- Co-auctioneer with John Barnes at the Jamaica basic School foundation Charity Ball, Nov 07
- Worked with Usain Bolt at the Great Northern Run after party May 2009
- Winner of West Midlands Women of The Year Awards & Inspirational Woman of the Year 2016
- Featured in the Daily Mail, The Mirror, BBC Radio, Lancashire Evening Post, Love It and Pick Me Up magazine

FOREWORD

"Through Adversity Breeds Success"

I first came across Mo at an womens empowerment event. The moment she spoke I could feel that she was passionate about supporting others to see beyond borders. Her mantra was to empower, equip and educate others and she showed an innate desire to not only give people the tools to improve themselves and their situation, but to show them how to. In this moment I knew Mo was exceptionally special in her drive, delivery and dedication. You could feel her aura of wanting to make a real difference in the world and to share her many entrepreneurial talents with others to help them excel.

It came as no surprise that she was writing a second book to help women share their unique stories with the world in order to inspire others. Sharing a story in the right way can be very powerful and life changing. It only takes that one person to be touched and then the ripple effect happens where more and more lives are positively being touched all from sharing a story. I myself know the importance of this after I shared my story about being brutally attacked and raped in my own home and the perpetrator received only three years in jail. Only the three people closest to me ever knew this happened as I like many victims allowed the perpetrator to make me have the all so common feeling of victims guilt where we would have shame. I never told anyone publicly what had happened to me for over a decade. One day I decided I no longer want to be the victim and I wanted to set myself free from it, so I shared my experience along with how I've come out the other side as a powerful Motivational Queen ® in a private facebook group and the response was positively immense. This allowed others to feel safe to share their story and many contacted me to say that after I shared my incident that they no longer feel the shame and the guilt they have suffered after their incidents. So I know how important it is to give women a platform to be able to feel safe to share their stories not only to help and inspire others but to set themselves free.

An amazing quality about this book is that it is borderless and reaches people from all over the globe. Mo really understands the essence that no matter who you are or where you come from, we all need a source of inspiration and you cannot this in any better way, than from real life stories with real life faces attached, which gives the book the true authenticity it deserves.

Within this book I'm sure that you will in some way or other relate to every single one of these women, even if you have not been in their situation, because you will know someone who has, or there will be elements in the story that resonate. The stories aid greater empathy and understanding about people, their circumstances, why they behave the way they do and hopefully bridge the gap of those that feel misunderstood on their life journey.

This is a real life grown up book that harnesses reflection to another level. There are many lessons and protection elements that can be gleaned from within the pages. The confirmation through reading that everyone is unique not only in their encounters but in the way they respond to them is educational within itself, and can make the difference in the way you know and view the mode of the world and your place within. The messages in the book go beyond reading the words and go to being within the words. You most undoubtedly will find it hard to put this book down once you start reading it as the stories are compelling, insightful, enlightening and inspirational.

By Zoe Bennett

Tales of Womanhood Vol 2

BRENDA DEMPSEY

Brenda Dempsey is a Survivor, Action Woman and Life Changer. From a young age (10) Brenda took **action** for starving children in Biafra, raising money and vowing she'd one day visit Africa and build a school. Brenda has recently returned from an entrepreneur expedition to Malawi.

As a **Survivor**, her Strength, self-belief and resilience were her armour when she found herself homeless with four children after her abusive marriage came to an abrupt end. Brenda's grit, determination and vision of a better life for herself and family were the staying power she needed to complete her B.Ed(Hons) degree during this arduous time to fulfil her childhood dream of becoming a teacher.

Transitioning is something Brenda embraces. After 25 years she left her beloved teaching to take up the challenge of **changing lives** and building a Revolution of 10 MILLION Spirited Leaders who are raising their Voices of Change, through writing, speaking and business. This creates a ripple effect, impacting change and providing extraordinary results for themselves, others and the world, through imagination, innovation and influence. Brenda is the founder of The VOW – The Voices of Women.

CHAPTER 1
THE VALUE OF YOUR GOLDEN THREAD
BRENDA DEMPSEY

"You see we are all diamonds, created from charcoal and the great pressures we endure in this life. "

When you are born as your umbilical cord is cut, an invisible thread connects those who are destined to meet, regardless of time, place or circumstance. This thread may stretch or tangle, but it will never break. Be open to each thread that comes into your life – the golden ones, even the coarse ones. You have the choice to weave them into a beautiful and brilliant life.

Life began for me one cold January evening in 1958. I entered this world to a very ordinary life; to a father who laboured and a resilient mother. We all lived in what was called a 'room and kitchen' in Clydebank, Scotland. There were my two elder sisters, one brother, my parents and me. By the time I was four we left Hamilton Street to pastures new in Dalmuir, to a flat with three bedrooms, a living room, kitchen and the luxury of an inside bathroom with a toilet.

I was a happy child. I became aware of something deep within me at the age of six. I had a strong desire to teach. Like many young children I would spend hours playing school – of course I was the teacher. This was the golden seed I would nurture for the next 30 years.

By the time I was ten, I knew there was a destiny bigger than I could ever imagine waiting for me somewhere in the future. What did a ten -year old know of the wider world? I lived in a world of play, school and loving life.

Until one day. I was struck like a rabbit in headlights at the burning images on the small black and white screen, that still haunt my mind today some 50 years on.

What I saw was my first experience of a world that caused and endured suffering, a suffering that no child should have to experience. These spine- chilling images were that of starving children from war torn Biafra in Africa. I was spurred into action. Within one week I created a 'jumble sale' and raised over £8 (a good sum of money, back in 1968). As a result, I found my name in the local paper for my efforts. I was accepting a golden thread that represented my compassion, protection and nurturing of defenceless children. Now I was weaving my golden thread tapestry between the teacher I longed to be and the need to empower children to learn how to be the best they can be. I was learning to be determined, driven and focused on achieving my dreams and goals, but I did this without a conscious mind.

A pivotal moment in my life was marrying at the tender age of seventeen. I naively left school without any qualifications, but a life had been carved for me that would teach me more valuable lessons than I could have learned sitting in a classroom. I had been exercising my determination, drive and focus once more. My golden thread was growing brighter. I had a mortgage. I was shopping for food instead of clothes. I was honing the trait of accepting responsibility. I was excelling in the workplace and had been promoted to a senior position of personal assistant to a director in the Singer Sewing Machine Company – the youngest ever. Most PAs were middle aged. I was 18.

By the age of 21 I had my first child, a daughter. I was

over the moon. I would do all the things with my child that my mother had not done with me. I would teach her everything, so that she would become great at what she chose to do. Eight months later I was pregnant with baby number two. How did that happen? I took this all in my stride and again was joyous at extending my family. More responsibility was put on my shoulders and I seemed to have the strength to do a good job and move forward. My golden thread was glistening even if I was not aware.

Fast forward another six years and I had grown from two children to four. Double trouble. Now life was beginning to get tough. The daily grind of looking after four children, running them to school, nursery and after school activities was wearing. Still I was building up my muscles of strength and stamina for what was to lie ahead.

My marriage was quite a rocky one due to my husband's jealousy and insecurities. Naturally, as a good catholic wife, I endured much of the abusive torture on a mental, emotional and physical level. This was the coarse thread that would create the crescendo I required further down the line.

Whilst all this was going on behind closed doors, to the outside world we were an idyllic family. You see, I had learned to adorn my battle armour on a daily basis. My protection was my sense of humour; my optimistic view of life and; my determination to never give up. Even though on this occasion I thought I was wrong. The lessons in life sometimes do not appear until many years later.

I was now in my thirties. Life was busy with the children when I was dealt another blow. My mother became ill with Lupus. This debilitating disease meant that was now running on a daily basis to care for her needs. I travelled a

26-mile round trip at least twice a day; sometimes three times. Still, I was super woman and I loved to cope with whatever came my way. Boy, this was definitely testing my resolve, resilience and respect for life.

It is in the darkest points of life that we build what we require to achieve bigger dreams. Even if we don't see it at the time, it soon unfolds beautifully when we are ready to awaken to a conscious state of living.

When my youngest child started school, I was finally ready to weave that unfinished golden thread of being a teacher. I was blessed to have an opportunity to go to teacher training and begin that wonderful, inspiring and fulfilling journey.

Of course, the path of enlightenment is never smooth. Why would it be? We are here to learn, grow and teach others. It was during the last year of my degree that my marriage finally fell apart. It was not a pretty end. It was violent and abrupt. I was engulfed with shame, guilt and sadness. How could this be? Still I had to move on. The saving grace and my driver was the achievement of my degree. I nearly never finished it, for I allowed myself to be consumed with grief, pity and hopelessness.

One day I found the courage, strength and determination to complete my journey. After all it was the key to my freedom and a better life for my children and me. I would be able to be the real, powerful and beautiful women that God intended. I had graduated this part of my journey with flying colours.

Life was great. I was able to be housed, buy a car and make decisions that benefited me and my family. One by one my children went to university and left home. WHAT? I was now an empty nester. Thank goodness for my work.

I was able to throw myself into it and strive to be the best I could possibly be. Giving my best most of the time was always my goal as being human, nothing is ever one hundred percent. Herein was another lesson. We can be too hard on ourselves. Perfectionism is a hindrance not a blessing as we can wrongly think. Experience as a teacher and manager taught me that 'good enough' is acceptable.

As my parents aged, it brought more responsibility. I loved my parents very much, but their health was deteriorating rapidly. My mother was now in a wheel chair for the Lupus had robbed her of the use of her legs. I was the main carer even though I worked as a teacher. I did not complain, after all they had given me everything. The thread during these years was very coarse and grew darker.

In 2004, my father, who had poor health since I was born, was the first of my family to die. Not a good experience to witness, suffice to say it caused three years of PTSD that I buried. It was not clear until many years later when I studied Neurolinguistic Programming and Timeline Therapy that I understood what I had experienced. Just over a year later my beloved mother passed away after spending the last ten months of her life in hospital. Plagued with infections she never spent time outside of the hospital. It was her new home.
I felt done.

This dark time was strengthening my resilience, my ability to carry on regardless. Creating a mindset that was beginning to learn how to control my emotions. Yet still I was not living a conscious life. All of this golden thread being woven unconsciously.
Three months after the death of my mother, my family endured the sudden death of my niece's fiancé. This

crushed my brother. Worse was still to come. Two years later we would lose a most precious gift. My niece's twenty- one- month old son lost a short, brave and bewildering battle with Krabbie's disease. This rapidly debilitating disease robbed him of his sight, hearing, movement and the unspoken word 'mummy' that my niece never heard.

The golden thread of all of these loses was the love that was evident within my family. We were indestructibly united and crushed at the same time. Battles were lost but many won and different roads taken because of them. This is a poignant lesson. A powerful lesson that we may never understand or see at the time, but one that reveals itself when the time is right.

Now, thankfully I had found a new love in my life after my mother died. A man who is kind, understanding and wants me to be happy. This blessing gave me the opportunity to leave my beloved Scotland. Something I never thought I would ever do. Hence the phrase, 'never say never' rings true. I moved to Surrey and created a new life for myself; a life that still involved teaching.

A new opening came in the guise of a Special Needs teacher in a Special School for Autistic children and young adults as well as those with speech and language difficulties. Now I could become the great teacher and leader that I envisaged ten years earlier. Now this darkened thread was ready to turn to gold once more.

A few years later, I was awakened to a wonderful world - the world of Personal Development. This new world whetted my appetite for something greater. A world that began to draw me in and open doors to expansive being, limitless possibilities and a world that I could create to serve others the way I had dreamt about when I was six years old.

Darren Hardy's book 'The Compound Effect' changed my life. Having always been interested in psychology and how the human psyche works, this book began to broaden my mind to what is possible when you are focused, driven and determined.

Bingo! The characteristics of determination, drive and focus are innate in me. They are my golden thread! This was a sign. This was my life. I had to find a way to live it. In October 2015 I handed my notice in. A day that I thought would never happen. I was taking a leap of faith and jumping from my childhood dream into a new world where I knew I was destined to make an impact. How, it was none of my business. I had to follow my dream and path.

January 2016 was the beginning of the life I live now. In three short years, I have founded a charity, written a book – Voices of Courage and now work as an associate publisher as well as in my private coaching business Diamond Success.

You see we are all diamonds. Created from charcoal and the great pressures we endure in this life. You are beautiful, yet flawed; priceless, yet feel unworthy and indestructible yet you feel fragile. Most of all when you find your purpose, passion and path you sparkle with such greatness that you become the beacon of light for others who need you.

It's when you are awakened that you are ready to look back at your path and see the dark and golden threads that make up the beautiful, bold and brave picture that is your tapestry of life. The value of this unique tapestry is priceless. My mission is to tell you how great you are, believe in yourself and find what you love and love what you do. YOU will rise like a phoenix after your darkness. Your golden thread evident as you blossom by being the best you can be in all that you think, say and do.

Be Brilliant

Tales of Womanhood Vol 2

HADASSAH ESTHER

Hadassah Esther is an author and founder of the Therapeutic Writing Group. She specialises in biographies and personal stories.

She is a Christian expressive writing therapist. She facilitates client's writing for self-exploration of specific issues. This includes a discussion of their writing to enhance self-awareness and personal growth. She encourages clients to write to express and explore what she calls the inner core, and to gain a deep sense of who they are, where they have been and where life is taking them. Hadassah offers a welcoming, accepting space to explore anxieties, challenges, celebrations and ethical issues of life in a flexible and original way

She specialises in using therapeutic writing techniques to aid personal transition and believes writing is transformational and has a healing power. She urges us to remember that therapeutic writing is not about the perfect literature piece of writing. It`s about the process of connecting and exploring inner thoughts and memories and finding meaning at an individual pace in a safe place.

CHAPTER 2
SCARS
HADASSAH ESTHER

"Pick up a pen, write about it and find meaning and healing."

The best people all have some kind of SCARS

By definition: scars are marks created during the healing of damage to the skin or tissues. A scar is a manifestation of the body's healing process. Scars are evidence of a wound. Most people have scars somewhere on or in their body. Most of the scars we receive are from something bad that caused injury, bleeding, and pain. What remains in time are scars that serve as reminders.

Just like grieving, there is no formula to healing when we have been wounded. I use writing to heal, in real life terms, what it means to go through a hidden heart as well as a physical healing process.

My story is about:

- **Beautiful Physical scars** which I have following a fatal car accident, injuries, hospital complications and eight operations.
- **Ugly heart scars** which I have from a disastrous abusive marriage of convenience and an abortion whilst I was maintaining a precarious outside sandcastle of keeping up social appearances. All the while, I was suicidal, broken and bleeding from internal heart and soul wounds.

There are a few choices and courses of action I could have and should have taken. I write about what I did, right or wrong, the results of those decisions, and how it changed the course of my life. I will pick up the story from that fateful night when a good girl went rogue....

One day, a couple of guys who also worked in the hospital came up to me and my friend and said they were going into town. They asked us to join them for a night out.

Heaven held its breath. The snare had been set, and I walked right into it.

Without giving it a second thought, we said, 'Okay, why not?'

After all, we were looking for a bit of fun and entertainment. To cut a long story short, neither of us had ever set foot in a nightclub before.

That night, I found myself in an unfamiliar environment. Without thinking, I had crossed over spiritual enemy lines. I sipped a drink that tasted horrid, but I maintained a straight face because I did not want to look immature and naïve in front of the men. Coca Cola in that place seemed to have its own strange taste.

'It's probably because it has been in the fridge for a few weeks. Hardly anyone ever orders Coke here,' they explained.

'Ah, that must be it,' I replied.   I am an adult; I can handle a coke, I thought.

One of the men took an interest in me. He offered to take myself and my friend back to our flat and then offered to see me to my room.

Heaven still held its breath.....

I had never 'been' with a man before. Sex and getting pregnant before marriage is not something I thought would happen to me. I assumed it was something I would never do. Here I was, not streetwise. I had ventured too far out into an unknown zone.

He was quite stunned and all he could say was,
'I am impressed; I didn't think virgins still existed.'

Heaven wept.....

I woke up the next morning with the hope that it was all some horrible dream, but the sheets told me otherwise. I gave myself away to someone I barely knew in a cheap hostel bed.

Terry had left. The realisation of what had happened hit me. I was burdened with guilt and shame. I became a different person.

I am a good girl, and good girls don't have one-night stands or whatever that was. What will the people at church have to say? What about my friends, my dad, my mum? Mother is going to kill me. I have let everybody down.

And then came the panic:
'Did he use protection?'
'Do people get pregnant the first time?'

'What if I contract HIV?'

I have failed; I have let everybody down. The logical solution I am going to have to take, is to marry this guy to make things right. I made another wrong decision.

What followed were the consequences of a one-night stand.

I was still in a position to choose, the next course of events in the following few months was still up to me.

I had started to build the Sandcastle. The wrong consultations gave wrong advice, made wrong decisions, and produced bad results.

I was pregnant. Curiously, Terry was neutral about it. He said, 'Well let's get married so you can have this baby.'

I did not want a baby. I barely knew the guy. I was not ready to be a mother, and most importantly, I was right in the middle of my academic course. Being pregnant meant automatic expulsion. My father would be devastated and disappointed.

Terry said, 'It's your choice. Whatever you decide, I will be with you. But it's your call.'

I went to seek advice from my aunt. She said;
'Why would you want to throw your life away over such a small matter? Your father doesn't have to know, get rid of it and finish college. If Terry wants to marry you, that's a

bonus! I will go and see your father about the wedding and arrange everything.'

Two weeks later after a back door visit to an abortionist gone wrong, the doctor finished the scan and said,

'You need urgent surgical treatment to remove remnants of the pregnancy and treat your septicemia.'

I spent a few days at the hospital. None of my family knew where I was. I lay septic in that bed and begged God to kill me. I could have died from multiple potential complications. I did get better in time and I went back to college. My parents had no idea what happened. In about six months and all in a blur I had an abortion and was now married.

I was healed physically, but something in me had died, my spirit light had been switched off.

By the time I graduated I was already pregnant again with my son. I was desperate for a child to reassure me I could still have children. I also thought having a son would make my husband happy and love me better. That was until the day I met my husband's mistress. I came home from work, and there was a woman with a baby in my living room! She refused to leave; he denied it was his baby.

She stayed the month, my husband's mistress, at my house. Yet every day, I put on a brave face, dressed up and went to work as usual. I never stopped going to church, dressing up, shopping, spending money and driving my husband's car.

My family in another town, never knew about it. The

secrets, the image, the lies, the appearances, the sandcastle had to remain intact, right?

There were three more years of emotional and psychological cat and mouse, before that final night when the police came. The questions, the examination, the baby crying, my mum shouting in the background and Terry ranting incoherently drunk.

The police lady was saying something; I could not comprehend what they were all saying. The police took him away that night. The next day I went to work, still trying to protect the image until the police turned up at work. They wanted to interview me and get my version of events, for the prosecution in court. I was a victim of domestic violence.

My workmates already knew anyway. They knew about the days I had to collect my son from nursery because his father had not, and that he switched off his phone the whole weekend. They knew from the nights when they would hide me at the back after Terry would turn up at my workplace in the middle of the night, drunk demanding to see me. My colleagues would then call hospital security to throw him out. Of course, I would be the subject of gossip in the staff room at tea time the next day.

The court prosecuted him for domestic violence; I declined to press charges. The judge imposed a six-month separation order. The sandcastle had collapsed. I could not stop it, and I just wanted to die. There was no going back. It was all over as painfully as it had started.

Now I did not want to be a single parent. I did not want to be divorced. I felt more hopeless, more powerless. As everything was taken away from me, the husband, the home, the money, the car, the material things. I felt lot of mental torture, self-condemnation, self-pity, and sadness crying myself to sleep, on the floor, with a bottle of pills in one hand, not brave enough to take them.

That was the morning when Jesus came and found me alone, broken and wounded.

The Holy Spirit woke me up;
'Why are you so angry?'

'Because he destroyed my life. He shouldn't have done what he did. And You did nothing to help me.'

It was not a dream, but a clear conversation. Just a peaceful, quiet presence is how I can describe it, and I heard clearly the following words:

'Your marriage was over before it began. Pick up a pen and start writing....'

'Write what?'

It seemed like the most random of instructions. But now I know what I was supposed to do: **Therapeutic Writing.**

Hadassah Esther, the writer was anointed. This was the point of transformation when I started writing. It took a few more months of being emotionally and spiritually resuscitated, and during this I just downloaded, it just started happening, and I started writing everything down.

I wrote about myself to myself, never intending to publish.

I wrote about my childhood sense of rejection and low self-esteem. The root causes of my decision-making processes became clear in retrospect.

I wrote about losing my faith. Faith is what I questioned about a God who would allow bad things to happen to a 'good' person like me. I was after all good, right? But I had to revise that justification in my decisions and contributions to what had indeed happened. Poor choices and bad decisions had actually happened to me. Accepting that was part of the healing journey of learning from mistakes.

FAST FORWARD: Revealing beautiful scars

After a long seven year journey of healing I remarried and had a baby girl. I decided to travel from our base in England to Mutare, a small town in Zimbabwe bordering Mozambique, to visit my husband`s parents.

On arrival in Zimbabwe, instead of waiting for the designated vehicle that was to take me to my final destination the next day, I impatiently decided to use public transport from the airport in Harare, all the way to Mutare where my in-laws lived.

I was moved at the last minute to the back, to give room to a husband and wife who wanted to sit together. The husband sat behind the driver by the window, in the spot I had sat. This was it! Death had set its trap; my seat itself was the snare, as I would later find out. As the bus left the city, I rested my head on my hand luggage on my lap and fell asleep.

I found out later that the vehicle had careered off the road less than forty miles from our destination. Myself and the man that swapped where I had been sitting were the two causalities, he died in the accident. I was thrown out head first through the back window, hit my head and was knocked unconscious. I had come out arms first because of my sleeping position thereby sustaining cuts from pieces of broken glass on my arms, and fractured my humerus in my arm. The skin had been ripped off the backs of both my arms from the shoulders and elbows. Everyone else walked out with only bruises or no injuries at all!

That accident was meant to take my life. My injuries were so severe that my mother-in-law had to bathe me. I was flown back to England and went straight from the airport to hospital for emergency surgeries. Complications and infections left me with scars on my head and arms.

At first, I disliked my physical scars; I even developed a daily routine of dressing up in front of a mirror; in garments with long sleeves, high necks, and used excessive face powder, way above my normal application. One day, as I was going through this routine, the Holy Spirit whispered;

'How long will you continue to hide your scars?'

' Well, the scars are hideous, and I feel ugly and even unattractive to my husband.' I muttered.

The next day, the same thing happened.

'For how long will you continue to hide your scars?

'Well Lord, cannot you see, everyone will stare at me and ask what happened...'

'For how long will you continue to hide your scars?' The Holy Spirit asked me again.

The third time, I paused and then realised, It was not the physical scars he was referring to, but the emotional and spiritual scars of the soul... I was being purposeful in hiding my now healed scars though. Besides, I was having flashbacks of the man who had died in the accident, and I kept asking God why He had spared my life.

'Why me? Why now? Why... again?' Sometimes we will never know or even understand. These '**why questions**,' can be used by the enemy to trap you into feeling guilty, having self-pity; depressed, let alone the idea that you are unimportant, unappreciated or unloved.

Eight operations later, I had stopped asking 'why me?' I asked for inner strength so that I was able to handle it. Maybe God wanted to use me as a testimony. Maybe I had to be the example of what God is able to do in an 'ordinary life.' Maybe I needed to be my own example.

I am who I am because of the emotional and physical scars. They have made me wiser, stronger and qualified me for my ultimate calling in life.

It turns out we all have sandcastles and scars in one form or another. There are not always right and wrong answers to what we choose to do with either. Now, I am a whole, healed woman. I am comfortable revealing my scars or hiding them to serve my mandate.

Some things about ourselves we hide, some we display and even show off. I just had to find my way of accepting mine and taking responsibility.

I forgave myself. I let go of the past.
I conquered my fears. I got healed, I got better.
I did not think I would find love. I did. I couldn't look at my reflection before, but now I embrace all my scars.

These are extracts from books **Hiding Ugly Scars** and **Revealing Beautiful scars.** I've used therapeutic writing about my experiences to help me 'go through it,' so I could let go and heal. I have been blessed with an amazing son who will always be part of my past, present and future. I had to confront my memories. I had to learn to embrace my scars both heart and physical.

My scars remind me that I did indeed survive my deepest wounds. They remind me that the damage life has inflicted on me has, in many places, left me stronger and more resilient. What hurt me in the past has actually made me better equipped to face the present. Life has to teach us some things. What have you learnt from the pain, how have the scars from your past helped you?

Tales of Womanhood Vol 2

Tales of Womanhood Vol 2

HEIDI MARJA

Heidi Marja Normann Einvoll, is 40 years old and a yoga instructor. Her technique helps people to learn to breathe again The rebreathing technique.

She is also an author and lives in The Northern Light country, Norway. In her book 'Følelseskarusellen', she shares her life story and her wisdom about life. The book is available in both Norwegian and English on Amazon.

Heidi has also been a co-author in the number 1 bestselling book 'The better business book,' which has been featured in Huffington Post. She has also contributed to the book 'Your heart matters.'

In her books she talks openly and authentically about her life and the struggles she had to go through to change her life completely.

Heidi wants people to wake up and be themselves, breathe deeply, follow their hearts and shine their light on others.

CHAPTER 3
WHEN THINGS CHANGE
HEIDI MARJA

"Life is all about change and it is changing all the time. The only thing that is constant is change."

It was new snow, a thin layer of snow on the ice. With my daughter Mariell, in one hand and a shopping bag in the other, I was on my way down a steep hill. I walked slowly down the hill so that I would not fall and hurt myself. Right next to me was my children's' playground. I heard children's' laughter and voices and noticed that my son Sindre was there playing. So, we took a shortcut over the playground because it was easier to walk there. We said Hi to Sindre, and then I stepped towards the road. That is when it happened. It was so icy, and because the snow lay like a blanket over the ice, it was like soap. I took a step on the ice, and I lost grip with my foot, falling from standing position, banging the back of my head into the ice and it felt like my head was going to explode. There was a cracking sound. It was so scary. There was a crunching sound in my head, and then it became totally black.

While I was lying there, I experienced the fall replayed in my head several times and my life passed before my eyes. It was an incredible, scary experience, and I thought I was going to die. I thought that my last hour was here. Luckily this was not the case, and this really was the turning point for my life.

Maybe you have also been there, where everything is dark around you, feeling like you are lying in a hole, not knowing how to get out or how you got there. You have stretched yourself to your limits, and you feel you can't be stretched anymore. Life seems desperate and dark.

This was how it was for me after my fall, where I had to start the whole process all over again. Destiny wanted it to be two days before I was sent to a rehabilitation centre for my injuries, and back issues. I went to the rehabilitation centre with my husband helping me on the plane, because I had no chance of making this on my own.

It was the best place I could have been sent to, because I had a severe concussion. I had to be checked on four times a day. The doctor said that I would think that I could do anything, but that my head would probably stop me when I couldn´t do it. For sure my head told me, not having an optimal functioning head makes you feel totally helpless. I was dizzy and bumbling.

To fall on the ice, and hit my head like that, was my worst experience, but also the best thing that could happen to me because I could start all over again with my life.

At first, I was so tired, because I was exhausted. I was exhausted from taking care of everybody else rather than myself. I had been giving and giving because I am a helper, and I really want people around me to feel good. My body got to relax and that is when one really gets to see the state of the body. Maybe you have noticed this when you have been working a lot, and when you finally get a day off, the body is exhausted, and you get the flu or catch a cold?

I had been taking it too far. I had helped others more than my capacity allowed. I had used all of myself up to the point that I had nothing more to give. I was diagnosed with ME and Fibromyalgia in addition to my injuries and back issues. The pain in my back was a sign that I needed to take more care of myself, and my injuries told me that I was going in the wrong direction. But I was listening to the signals my body, through pain was sending me. It was saying that it was time to calm down, to take it easy. It was time to listen to what my body really needed. Pain is a sign that something's wrong, and that there is an imbalance in the body. In addition, I had zero energy.

In my case, I had been rushing between my dad, my sister, and my work. I only had time to speak to friends when I sat on the bus on my way home from work. Then there was housework and falling asleep on the couch before doing it all over again the next day.

It was no wonder that I was always sleeping, or that I had to fall on the ice and hit my head to get the reminder I needed about life, and how I had been driving myself into the ground. At that time, I was a mom of two children, stressing from one thing to another, and everything had to be perfect on the outside. Maybe you recognise this within yourself? You may be stressing from a desire to manage all the expectations and demands that you think others have of you.

But then it really is just you that puts these crazy impossible demands on yourself, things that you can't possibly achieve. Then your body screams to you to calm down!

Instead of calming down and treating my body the way I should have done, I relied on strong painkillers from my doctor. They were so strong they could probably have been given to a horse. I used them because I was in such pain that I could not walk properly.

Filling your body with painkillers is not always the solution. Many use painkillers, antidepressants and anxiolytic drugs. This is something I think could be cut in half if people learned to listen more to their bodies and to listen more to themselves, to love themselves for the person they are.

It is too bad that so many young people use medication, especially antidepressant drugs. Much of this comes from stress and high pressure according to research, from putting high demands on ourselves, as it was in my case.

Did you know that 80-90 percent of people that go to doctors in Norway do so because of stress and stress related diseases? The numbers show the same around the globe. There is a Japanese researcher that has found out that there is only one real disease and that is stress. He has done his research on Japanese workers and found out that all other diseases are associated with stress. I strongly believe this. In my case stress was probably a huge part of why I had pain and struggled with little energy.

The road to improvement for me was that I understood that I needed to calm down. I learned to meditate and listen to soothing words. I understood that how my body was feeling was a result of the life I had been living. The pain and the knots in my body were feelings that I was stuck. There were situations that I had not processed and that I had tried to shut the lid on.

Many people do that, they put a lid on their feelings and emotions, and move on. But the fact is that when you don't look at the situation, when you don't go into the feelings and process it all the way, they get stuck inside the body. You will experience it again and again, until you look at your thoughts. If you push them away, they will come up in front of you again and again until you take a look and do something about them.

It is also true that thoughts make stress, particularly

thoughts about not being good enough, or not pretty enough etc. You are beautiful and unique just the way you are. The ability to love myself was buried deep in me. I hated myself. I couldn´t understand why my body wouldn´t work as it should. Sometimes I was so sick, and my pelvis locked itself, so I had to use my crutches or wheelchair to get anywhere.

It has been a long journey to start all over and find myself again, and get to know myself and to love myself for who I am. I found my heart, when I dared to go inside myself and feel. When I dared to really take up the fight. Because when you change, the outside forces and people around you will start to wonder. They are used to you being somebody that has no needs. You have been there for others and not seen your own needs. Suddenly you tell them that things are not ok anymore. You set your boundaries and you work systematically to do what is best for yourself.

I told my husband when I understood that I had to make these changes that I would not be doing certain things for a month. I would not do any housework. There were some protests, but luckily, he accepted it and he is happy with it all now. Luckily, I have a kind and understanding man who made it possible for me to do this. I have cut out all the medication that I had been using over several years because I believed so strongly that this was the way to get well, to cooperate with my body, my soul and my spirit, at the same time.

At first, I got sicker, and I got very sad and depressed, because I understood how I had treated myself, and I understood that my way to recovery was through getting to know myself all over again.

I had been through years of hell in pain and to cut

painkillers out and feel the pain was a suffering, but also necessary to start the process of getting to know myself. The pain and the knots in my body told me about the life that I had been living. They told me about violence in my childhood home. They told me about always having felt different, and that I was bullied for it in school. It told me about disease, and it told me about sorrow, also, that I had used my body as a garbage bin instead of letting all these feelings go.

What also happened when I went through this journey into the mysteries of the body was that I discovered myself. I found the heart of who I really, truly am. I found my capabilities as a healer. I found out that I could help people in a different way. That I could help people to open up and discover the treasures that are lying hidden in their hearts, under all their suppressed) feelings, and under all their thoughts built on fear.

I also found my courage, my strength and my truth. I found what was true for me. I found my authentic self. Not what I thought I was, but who I felt I was. I found out that I could give with my heart, and not be stripped of energy, but instead be filled up with energy. I also found my joy for writing. I found out that I have a writer inside me, and that I loved to convey and share my mission and what my dreams are. Not the dreams of others, but my dreams. All this had been lying latent in me all these years.

I started to open up, exploring deeper inside myself, daring to get to know who I truly am, daring to look at what had limited me and held me back, to look at all my fear and all the resistance that had built up in myself, and all the untruths that I had told myself. We are our own worst enemy, and it is mostly ourselves that put boundaries and restriction on ourselves. We look at ourselves as small and insignificant.

The truth is that we are much stronger, more powerful and have more courage and strength than we think. When I opened myself up to living from the heart, I got more done in six months than I had done in six years, because I did it with the whole of me. I had my energy with me, and I created it from my heart.

Now I earn a living from my own company. Financially things go up and down, but that is how it is with one's own company. It is not always a bed of roses, but I live from what I love. I am happy, and I have a good life because I follow my heart. I have a goal and I have a dream.

Do you have a dream? Have you found what your passion is? Do you do what you love to do, or do you do it because it gives you a pay check and food on the table? Are you like I was, doing the same over and over again, day in and day out, feeling that something is missing, but not knowing what, and doing nothing about it, wondering what you can do?

Now I live my dream. I live every day doing what I love. I pop out of bed to get the children to school, then I take a yoga session because I have found that yoga is a great start to the day and helps me to let go of everything and then I am ready to go. It's is a calm start on the day. I eat breakfast and get into my office and start my working day. Maybe I will be writing a new book like I am doing now, or, having conversations with my customers and some of my mentees. I am in flow and in alignment.

Falling on the ice was a wakeup call for me. It was my way of starting my new journey. My true journey where I do what I love to do. What I am passionate now is teaching people to understand what an amazing instrument they are. We need to listen to our bodies. Our bodies give us signals all the time. Often, they give signals that something is wrong, that something needs to change. Many people live in the past, and don´t see that life has moved on. This was also the case for me. I had bypassed my thoughts and feelings.

I tell you this so that you understand that you don´t need to be stuck in your past. You don´t need to be a victim of your circumstances, of things you have done in your life or experienced. You can take a look at your life and see that your life has moved on and you can decide today that you want to make a change and start creating your dream life. We create our lives based on the choices we make and that is what defines the life we live.

Life is all about change and it is changing all the time. The only thing that is constant is change. That is why it is important to look at you own life. Are you living your life to the fullest?

When I woke up after falling on the ice, I soon realized that life is too short to not live life to the fullest. To fall like that was the best that could have happened to me, because I found myself. Now it is your turn to follow your dream!

Tales of Womanhood Vol 2

HONOURABLE MP MEMORY MBONDIAH

Memory is a politician in Zimbabwe under the Movement for Democratic Change Alliance party. She won an award as The Best Woman Leader in MDC Alliance in 2017.

She studied Global Youth Work and acquired principled negotiating skills at the Open University in 2005 and is currently studying Psychology with the University of Unisa Zimbabwe.

She is a hardworking single mother to two astounding children. Her youngest recently scored 15 points at A level and is waiting to take up a place to do Medicine at the University of Zimbabwe in Harare.

She enjoys swimming & travelling.

CHAPTER 4
THE JOURNEY TO SHEROE
HONOURABLE MP MEMORY MBONDIAH

"My life soon became a living hell especially with my involvement in politics everyone around me feared for their lives "

Early years with dad

Growing up, l was the eldest of four girls in my family. My father was a respectable man, in his role as a superintendent of the police force. In the days when l grew up, a superintendent commanded a great amount of respect from the wider family and community. As the eldest in my family expectations naturally came nicely packed with the title. My father had high expectations of me and my sisters, so he invested a great deal of time in our education. He lectured us consistently on why it was of paramount importance to be educated to the level of being a teacher a nurse or a doctor, as these professions did not expire. He would often highlight that men soon got bored of an uneducated woman, opting for the woman with an education as opposed to, before his time, where women were expected to plough the fields and bare children.

I didn't realise at the time, that my father was in the process of empowering me for what was to come.

Then, I felt, he was an old man with high expectations for his daughters, and that l was really not equipped to be a teacher or a nurse. Those professions just didn't appeal to me funnily enough. I took up karate lessons at my school instead and won myself a few belts as l was extremely fascinated by the sport as a whole and sometimes used the techniques on my little sisters when they did not conform to what I said. I soon became known for my flying kicks in the house, when order was not maintained.

With time I realised that karate would not be something that I could use to earn a living in Zimbabwe, especially at this time when the economy was starting to dwindle with programmes like ESAP (Economic structural adjustment programme) on the agenda for the country. This was one of the significant changes to the economy of Zimbabwe. As a teenage then, it was much apparent, that men took the decisions within the family, at school board meetings, on TV and in politics.

Although this concerned and bothered me and caused my mind to ponder, I was still too young to comprehend things fully.

My darkest hour

Mom and dad long separated, but I remained in the custody of my father. I kept in touch with mom during the holidays when I would spend time with her. I had heard that mom had not been well, but little did I know that her life was nearing the end. Had I known, I would have given her one more big hug. To me she was a young woman and I guess I had never experienced the death or a loss of a loved one, so I did not expect to hear the worst.

It was Valentine's Day that her life gave way, and for me this was my darkest hour and the beginning of the long walk in life. The death of my mom left me broken and shattered to say the least. I was left hopeless with a bitter taste in my mouth.

By the time of mother's death I too had traditionally married my then sweetheart to my father's distress, as his dream of seeing me graduate had come tumbling down. For my husband and I, our life was good together, we had a daughter but with mom gone I knew things had to shape up for the better. So, with a job in a travel agent I started a family and my life as a woman.

The shift

With a young family to feed, life was not all roses, as things were getting harder by the day in Zimbabwe. Emigration had already started to increase with many people leaving for the likes of UK, South Africa and other countries in search of a better life. This included very close family members who had all eloped to neighbouring countries to study or seek better opportunities or what they called the 'greener pastures.'

At this point, my husband was working in a good company, so moving away was not on the cards for us and this would have severely threatened our marital bliss so the decision to leave was never a preferred option.

The cost of living was extremely high, and many young people were jobless despite any level of education. This angered me as I remembered my father's words and his guarantee that with an education life would be a lot better.

I had enrolled in a night school in an attempt to better my career prospects. What I saw on the ground didn't give me the assurance that I too would enjoy a good career one day in my beloved country Zimbabwe. To me, this was not the case. In fact, many individuals were worse off even with an education, there were no jobs to be found.

The sight of homeless women and children around the railway and under bridges became a serious eyesore for me. I kept asking why the current government was not doing something about it. On the other hand, the main opposition party was spreading like a wild fire. I once heard that, 'Leaders are people who activate change and cannot wait for change to happen.' This knowledge made me realise immediately who l was and where l belonged. I wanted to be part of the change to the former bread 'Basket of Africa' to my Zimbabwe. I felt I owed it to my people to do something about the problem.

With this self-conviction, I joined the **Movement For Democratic Change** at the tender age of 20. I had so much zeal to be part of this big movement and be amongst like-minded young men and women. My God, I was inspired.

Setbacks

Trouble came, as the government was not happy about the new developments. Word soon went around that l had become one of the new converts. There was no rest for the opposition, as people were being victimised, arrested or tortured for no apparent reason. I remember one time, we were beaten and arrested several times for demonstrating against price hikes.

My life soon became a living nightmare, especially with my involvement in politics.

My marriage was now under threat with strained relations with my husband who needless to say also feared for his life. I moved my children to boarding school and left my home in an attempt to hide for my life's sake.

The media did not spare me as most papers were controlled by the ruling party.

As election time drew nearer the real challenge began. Then

men felt that as a woman, I had right to be in a leadership position and others thought I had no capacity to survive an election.

Many men in the party also attacked me and asked why a woman was in politics. Continuous frustrations continued to arise and disrupt me and my agenda. At one point. I woke up to a media massacre of lies about me, my name was everywhere. They were attempting to tarnish my image and make me stand down.

By this time, I was isolated as my family had significantly detached from me, with most of them asking what and why I was involved in politics. I had no financial or emotional support from my family at all. Consequently, I ran for election with zero budget and of course I lost.

I was devastated; however, I did not lose hope. I was determined to succeed one day.

In 2008 it was election time again. The reign of terror that was unleashed upon the opposition party was horrendous. Together with other women we started penetrating the rural areas of Zimbabwe, campaigning at full force. We never stayed in one place for too long though, in case the regime caught up with us.

By now it was a serious crime to support the opposition. The torture and beatings continued, I had never seen so much bloodshed in my life. I can still visualise my colleagues who were also victimized for supporting the opposition. Some didn't make it sadly, RIP. We would go for several days without bathing or eating a proper meal. I remember vividly a woman in Mashonaland central province (which is a party stronghold), her home had been burnt with her husband and two sons in the hut. She ran for her dear life and was now living by the river pretending to be mad just to save her life. The rest is painful history.

I stood again for election. Though I thought I had grown smarter, the competition was even tougher. I was called all sorts for standing for what I believed in. I wanted to a part of the women making meaningful changes in my country. No one really wanted to be around me. I missed my children and my husband was now living with another woman. After all the hard work I lost again. It was such a blow, I was literally a laughing stock. My family continued to isolate me in fear of their own lives and being accused by the regime of harbouring an enemy of the state.

At one point, I decided to run to neighbouring South Africa. I stayed there undocumented for a year. The pictures of my fellow comrades that I saw on the news were devastating. I thought that I had been a coward by running away and decided to go back.

Upon return, I was homeless and decided to go back to my father's farm to raise capital and start again. l moved towns as the cost of living was too high and l could not afford to live in the capital city of Harare and besides, my life was still threatened due to my political affiliation with the opposition party.

I started a chicken project in an attempt to stabilise myself. Although my inner voice kept me alive, l was almost on the verge of a breakdown at all levels.

My biggest devastation followed, I lost my best friend and sister Ronia Bunjira to cancer. She was very a strong woman who had walked with me along this lonely journey of Politics MHSRIP.I literally broke down with no one to turn to. I felt the need to keep pushing against all odds.

Another Try

Leading up to the 2018 election, I remember the hard work involved in the campaigning efforts as this time we didn't know what to expect. We had lost **the Opposition Leader and his vice.** The events leading up to the election promised or almost guaranteed a triumphant victory. The speculation was high, with lots of expectations for building a new Zimbabwe.

While waiting impatiently for the results, my heart was beating from right inside my mouth. When they started announcing the results, I could clearly see that it was possible that the overall result had been rigged again, but just after midnight, my daughter came running to my bedroom, my name had been announced, I had won. Today I stand a proud member of the parliament of Zimbabwe. But, it's not over until it's over. The journey continues.

Tales of Womanhood Vol 2

Tales of Womanhood Vol 2

MICHELLE NWOSU

Michelle studied Psychology and Sociology in the Seychelles before coming back to the UK.

She has a 'Certificate in Mortgage Advice and Practice,' and has 10 years' experience in the banking industry. Michelle began as a cashier and later became a Mortgage Manager and a Financial Advisor, before she left to become a full time Home-Maker.

Michelle is a devoted wife and mother. She home schools her children and is the owner of MichBakes, her homebased baking business that she runs along with her husband. They specialise in 'Free from' (gluten, wheat, soya and dairy free) cakes for all occasions. She is in the process of getting her first book published.

Michelle lives in the UK with her wonderful husband Douglas and their five children. She is an active member of her church community and teaches at the Sunday school.

Having been abused at a very young age and treated like trash, she is passionate about seeing people set themselves free from things that have bound them in fear. Her faith in God is what keeps her going.

CHAPTER 5
TRASH TO TREASURE
MICHELLE NWOSU

"You do not have to fight this alone, as there is a God who loves you, and His name is Jesus. He died so that you and I can live again. "

Some of us are walking around with half a smile pretending that all is well. No one can see our scars, because they are emotional, mental, financial and sexual, hence they are hard to detect and to be considered as abuse. These scars are not visible to the naked eye, they are so deep within and not physically noticeable. Some of us have been bullied and tortured with words, mentally and emotionally. So today we feel ashamed about how we look. We feel too skinny, too big, not pretty enough, too tall, too short, not good enough, and the list goes on and on.

Our self-esteem has been wrecked by negative words that have been spoken to us. Words that have cut so deep that if exposed will make us vulnerable. How many of us have been abused in ways, whichever shape or form that have caused us to be too scared to walk the street. I have been abused in so many ways and I was scared to walk the street, fearing my own shadow. My advice to you, is do not keep silent about your abuse. Get out of that abusive relationship and give your heart, soul, mind and body a chance to heal. Stop living in silence; let us break the chain of fear.

I am more than a conqueror, through Jesus Christ who gives me strength. I am no longer bound by my oppressors. I did not wear my scars physically but mine were wounds deep within my soul. I thought no one would ever love me, but the truth is that there is life after abuse. I know by telling my story I am exposing myself, but I am willing to be selfless in order that I may save another. I want to encourage and ignite your soul with Faith and Hope. There is an abundant life awaiting you. I want to comfort you, to let you know that there is hope. You do not have to fight this alone, as there is a God who loves you, and His name is Jesus. He died so that you and I can live again.

I was raised in an extended family ranging from my grandparents, to my aunty and uncles and cousins, plus my four siblings. There were fifteen people under one roof. Crazy I know, but I could not change the family to whom I was born into and I could not change the circumstances of my upbringing. The atmosphere was very deprived, miserable, broken and filled with continuous domestic violence.

I was born in the UK, in Birmingham, but before I was two years old, my mother moved back to the Seychelles with me, to live in the place where she originally came from. I hated going home after school. There was a lack of love, and attention. As I was growing up, my mother was a gambler and because of her addictive habits, I went to school most of the time without food to eat, because she spent all her monthly salary gambling. Sometimes she would be so broke that she could not afford to buy clothes for me. All her anger was geared towards me, after she had lost her money fulfilling her addiction. She treated me as if I was just a hassle to her.

I had to grow up very fast, because at a very young age I was given responsibilities to cook, clean and to skip school to help look after my siblings. I cannot remember having a childhood, because for me all I have ever known was house chores, cooking and looking after babies. Life was hard, stuff happened, everyday a fight would break out between my mother and the rest of the family members. They would use all sorts of weapons to hurt each other with and at a young age I watched these horrific incidents happening before my very eyes. Naturally, these incidents deeply affected me. So many times, I thought of committing suicide. I was treated like a servant. Each time I asked for five rupees which is equivalent to 0.29 pence in Sterling, I was told that I had to work for it, cooking, cleaning, and ironing.

From the age of nine, one of my uncles sexually molested me, until the age of 12. I remember that day very vividly, from the date to even what I was wearing. It was 1988 the day of the Assumption according to the Catholic Church calendar. Since it was a tradition, the schoolchildren were obligated to attend church. My mother took me to church, left me there, and told me that she would pick me up after the service. When it was time to be picked up, my mother was nowhere to be found, instead she sent my uncle to pick me up. I asked him where my mother was, and he told me that she was gambling at her friend's place. I told him that I would like to be with her.

He reluctantly took me to where my mother was. When she saw me, she was furious and verbally abused me, telling me to get out of her way, that I should not come to disturb her peace and if she loses her money I will be dealt with in a harsh way. I was scared so I obeyed. She told my uncle to help me get dressed. Therefore, he took me home, and there was no one at home at the time, so he used the opportunity to sexually molest me. He told me that no one will believe me if I dare expose him. So, this abuse continued until I was 12 years old, until one day when my teacher started talking to us about not allowing anyone to touch us inappropriately and that we should have the courage to tell an adult if we feel we are being molested. That was the day that I decided to tell my grandmother about it, and she told me to swear to secrecy that no one should know about it, not even my mother, otherwise if I caused trouble for my uncle I would be thrown out of the house with my mother and siblings.

Although I did not talk about it, I took matters into my own hands and one day while I was in the kitchen, I took a knife and I pointed it at my uncle and told him that if he did not stop abusing me, I would kill him. That was the day he stopped touching me, but he never stopped looking at me with his lustful eyes. For me to stay living in the same house, seeing my abuser every day and pretending that nothing had ever happened was absolutely absurd and ridiculous, but at that time I felt that there was no way out. Who do I trust?... who do I turn to at such a young and vulnerable age? By the time I was 18 I confided in my aunty about what happened to me and she told me that she believed me because this uncle had a history of previous molestation of other family members.

At the age of 21, I found out that I was not supposed to have been born, that I was the result of a failed abortion. My mother felt it was appropriate to tell me this, one day in front of my friend. I remember that day as if it was today. I remember the smile on her face as she callously made the comment. I have forgiven her but sticks and stones can break my bones, and these words surely did break my heart and leave a lasting impact on my memory.

I escaped my reality through daydreaming. I used to see myself being better than I was. I have always tried to prove myself by working so hard, to achieve a better life. At the age of 18, I started seeing myself going downwards on a spiral of promiscuity. I went into that lifestyle because I wanted to be loved, and it felt right at the time and made me feel accepted. I was always looking for someone to love me. I was an easy target for my predators. At the age of 20 I got involved with a narcissist, who was twice my age. I looked up to him as if he was my dad. What started as a friendship soon became a toxic relationship. I was soon to realise the brutal reality of how possessive and jealous this man was. He sniffed my clothing to ensure that I was not going out with other men. I found myself trapped in a so-called love- hate roller coaster each day from tenderness to torment, I had enough. I felt trapped; I could not escape due to my fear of him. He gave me everything that money could buy and deep down I was always looking for a way out. At the time, I was working and was still living at home, so he isolated me from my family and friends by getting me rented accommodation so that I could be on my own. It was an adulterous affair, he was married with three children and although I knew adultery was a sin, he told me that I should not be stupid, that he was the one committing adultery and not me. I was so naive and believed everything he told me.

He knew that I did not have a male protector around me to defend me, because through my friendship with him I had shared all my struggles with him. He knew that I did not have a father to stand up for me. I was an easy target to be manipulated and abused mentally, emotionally, physically and sexually. I was so co-dependent on him and it was a very unhealthy relationship. I accepted everything he did to me because I thought I did not deserve better, I felt secure, I felt taken care of and there was a price to pay. I attributed the abuse as love. I was scared to break away, I thought no one would ever love me.

He criticized me, belittled me, and made me feel unworthy. He made me feel that I was not attractive enough and that he was the only man who was good for me. He constantly compared me to his wife, expected me to behave like her, cook and iron like her. I felt trapped in my sin of not knowing who I was or what I had become. I did exactly what was expected of me. He told me that it was my fault if he got angry; he told me that his love for me was what caused him to beat me up and spit in my face. I lived in pretence to maintain the perfect image. I was his property, his possession. I was expected to just serve him, his ego, and all his sexual demands at any time and any day. The sex was not enjoyable; in fact, it was wreaking emotional havoc within me.

I was a slave to him. I was forbidden to have friends and he even got people to watch my every move. I was terrified of staying in the relationship, but I was also afraid to leave because he had shown me his revolver previously and warned me that if I ever left him, he would kill me. I had two abortions, as I did not want to bring children into this world with a narcissist. I felt ashamed and guilt overwhelmed me. I thought that I would never be able to have children and thought no one would ever love me with all my past sins. I felt that my life was over, there was nothing to live for and I was not even 25 at that time. I fell into deep depression, and hopelessness and loneliness became my friends.

At the age of 22, I made a decision to leave the Seychelles and to settle in the United Kingdom. I thought that this would solve all my problems, but how naïve was I. I moved to a new country, but I carried my problems with me. Instead of leaving him, I kept in touch and carried on a long-distance relationship. His control over me did not stop, in fact it got worse. He would turn up any time unannounced at my doorstep. One day he sat me down and told me that he had planned my death. He told me how he was going to kill me and that no one would ever suspect him as the murderer. He tore my clothes, poured red wine on me, and told me that was how he would make my blood spill. Fear gripped me with the thoughts of my life ending. I cried myself to sleep. I was in a dark place and I felt all alone.

My happy moments came when I ran to God. One day I decided to pray by faith. I needed God to change my brokenness to wholeness. I needed His intervention. I was stuck and I was desperate for a saviour with eyes that could see my situation, a saviour with ears that can hear my plea, a saviour with hands that can reach down and deliver me. I asked God to reveal Himself to me. That same day I will never forget, He sent a lady, Sister Monica my way to talk to me about Jesus. She told me everything that I had asked God that day in my prayer. She invited me to church the following Sunday and God answered my prayer and saved me. This was April 2004, when I became a believer in Jesus Christ. At that moment, I decided that I would take action and change my address again. I packed and moved to a new address. As terrified, as I was, I knew I had made the right choice.

God has now blessed me with a wonderful husband. He

has been the only man who has loved me and not treated me as an object. He proposed to me within six weeks of us becoming friends and he told me that he would make an honourable woman out of me. He did not believe in sex before marriage, so we waited until our wedding day to consummate the relationship. We are now 13 years into our marriage with our five wonderful children. I thought no man could ever love me. The devil is a liar. No human being has the right to make you feel unworthy. I have cried so many tears, but I am now in a place of rejoicing. It does not matter about your past, nor your current situation. God has the ability to heal our past. He is the one that gives me my identity, my strength and He affirms me. He is so awesome. The God that I serve specialises in using trash and transforming it into beautiful treasure.

Tales of Womanhood Vol 2

RACHEL TRACEY

Rachel is a Maths Teacher and a Biomedical Scientist. Aside from these things, her passion is to motivate young women to love themselves and make choices that are beneficial for the outcomes they wish to see in their lives. She believes in challenging beliefs and success limiting thoughts.

Rachel was a co-author in Volume 1. in which she wrote about a 'transition from a place of self- hate to a place of self-love.' Following on from this she released a preview book of the story 'you are the first and the best.' She is in the process of writing the complete version.

Rachel is an active part of her church community where she teaches Sunday school and delivers the word to the congregation

Rachel views her biggest achievements to date as trusting in God and getting to know and accept herself; a journey that she is still on and in fact hopes to remain on so that she can be a blessing to others on their journeys.

CHAPTER 6
DUST YOURSELF OFF AND TRY AGAIN
RACHEL TRACEY

"You are the first and best version of yourself"

What happens when disappointment comes your way? When that dream or vision crumbles before you? When the very thing you know was sent to elevate you leaves you lower than ground zero...

What happens when you choose what you think is right for you and instead of leaving you in the perfect Utopia, you get left in what seems, what feels like total and utter disarray. How do you handle that? Heart break, failed business relationships, failed friendships, strained family relationships. How do you handle it?

How do you! YOU! who are so filled with purpose, end up doing things so far from your calling, from your destiny? How do you end up so close to destiny, yet so far away? How do you, who perhaps has never even dreamt of being an athlete, end up running all the time? Is there something that you need to face? I invite you to DUST YOURSELF OFF AND TRY AGAIN.

In volume one of this wonderful series of stories, I told of my experiences of low self-worth in the story 'Transition from self-hate to self- love.' In the quest to dust ourselves off and try again, it is important to continuously keep in mind that we are the first and the best version of ourselves. That we as individuals are created AS WE ARE, UNIQUELY designed to fulfil our carefully thought out plans and purpose. In a way that only we can. That is a fact that doesn't change just because we make a mistake or face disappointment. Hold on to and keep in focus your identity. You are who you are in spite of prior, or even current situations.

I want to present the notion of dusting yourself off to you by considering the choices that we have made. Sometimes we think that we know what we want or need without truly considering the consequences of our actions or even if we were meant to be in the place where we have chosen to be in the first place. I for one have been in situations, more than I care to admit, whereby the poor choices I made, have impacted me in so many ways that I had not even thought were possible. In ways that I have not even yet realised. Whilst we do not hold all of life's answers, it is important to remember that we ought to carefully consider the impact that we may be having by considering the things that do not occur to us naturally to consider.

For example, I never dreamed that by virtue of wrong association, the very thing that had been so divinely handed to me could be snatched away in an instant. When you are called into a place, you must remember the purpose for which you were called there.

By wrong association in a recent venture, I found myself in a position whereby I was paying the price for a 'crime' not committed by me. It was my time, I had been called forth to partake of something that I had thought about and meditated on. Something that had been in my heart. I let my guard down to the wrong extent and ultimately 'forgot' that there was a reason for me pursuing the opportunity handed to me. Moreover, I let the actions and the outcome wrought by another, hold me captive. Though matters were ultimately out of my hands, I have had to accept responsibility on my part in order to move forward; something that we must practice if we are to level up and keep moving from strength to strength. Something that we must master in order to dust ourselves off and try again.

There I was, full of potential, opportunity fulfilled, deal closed. Yet there, mixed in with the pot of fresh success, was a bitter root. A root that was derived from disappointment in another individual, but most of all disappointment in myself for having any involvement with that person; for stepping in heart first, mind last. A root that almost caused me to throw the whole pot away.

What I have learned though is that rather than throwing the pot away, there are things that you can instead add, to eradicate the bitter root.

What things have left you feeling bitter? What is it that you have not forgiven yourself for? I encourage you to take responsibility and ownership, forgive yourself and MOVE ON.

DUST YOURSELF OFF

Admittedly there are deeper and darker things than wrong association that I have had to shake off of me (spells of doubt, fear, anxiety and depression for example), but I want you to know that there is power in the choices that you make, choices that you didn't even know were yours to make. I implore you to take a magnifying glass to the finer details of your life and consider those things that you wouldn't usually; challenge the thoughts that you usually have. The thoughts that you have been having for the past year, or years, maybe even decades. Start to shine a light on the things that you may be afraid to face, or that you may have never even realised needed addressing. Dust yourself off.

Let's consider and explore the opening questions of this story. What does happen when disappointment shows itself?

For me, when I learned that the thing that I had dreamed of having dried up, my response was to feel a sense of sorrow on the inside. This was swiftly followed by a plight of avoidance. I refused to sit and think things through. I started playing the blame game. I started to make decisions irrationally. I tried to gain success swiftly without giving any deep thought to what I was doing. The trouble with my response is that I let disappointment push my mind into the wrong type of overdrive. Sure, I was and am still successful in my own right, but the mentality I adopted took me to a place whereby I became pessimistic instead of taking the lesson I had learned and using it as a stepping stone in the right direction. The dangerous thing is, I thought I was doing the right thing and was persuaded that I had the correct mindset, this sent me full steam ahead in the wrong direction.

I encourage you in the face of disappointment, not to act irrationally, but rather to gain clarity in your thinking before making another move. My mistake was that before dusting myself off appropriately, I tried again. Don't make the same mistake. What is for you is yours and will inevitably manifest itself in your life. The time that you try to save by cutting corners can cost you far more time than you had ever anticipated.

How did I feel?

Indeed, as suggested by the opening sentences, the dreams that I had crumbled, I felt low within myself for a while and confused. In disarray, I had been certain as to how things should have turned out and unprepared for the possibility that something may go wrong or not to plan as it were. I had no contingency. The saving grace for me in that time is that whilst I was partially consumed by disappointment, it was just that: 'IN PART.' Due to the other responsibilities and roles that I had undertaken, I still had a sense of purpose, success and validity. That didn't change the fact though that I needed to have thought carefully, meticulously, intentionally; about the different circumstances surrounding the goal that lead to disappointment. Contingencies are not signs that you do not believe in the vision, rather they are evidence of the thought process surrounding what you are doing. Had I thought of some of the things that led to me feeling disappointed, I would have been better prepared not to act on impulse, but rather in wisdom.

How did I end up so up close and personal to what I saw as a part of my purpose, yet with such a taste of bitterness? Again, I reiterate that it is in preparation and with careful thought that you secure your dreams and goals. I was in the right place at the right time but took it for granted that those who were around me also were. We see that 'association' word come back into play here as I make it clear that failure to keep my eyes on the prize and an urge to feed social desires, that were secondary to the main purpose at hand, lead to me almost missing out. ALMOST?

ALMOST!

I say almost because I came to the point where I realised that there were indeed ingredients that I could add to the pot of success that had been previously contaminated. That pot mentioned earlier, that had been tainted by the bitter root. What are those ingredients that we can add to restore the success to its former glory and beyond?

A <u>pinch</u> of reflection: Dare to think about the disappointment that you may well have compartmentalised in your mind by now. Not overthinking, reflecting. How were things? How are things going to be from now? What part did you play? What part WILL you play next time? There's nothing wrong with reflection, which is a crucial part of the self-evaluation process, it makes for a tasty soup of success.

Next you will have to turn the heat down a little AND remove the lid for a while: In your life, let there be release, let the pressure be reduced. Forgive yourself and others. Take the limits off. Who says you can't rise again? **A <u>jug</u> of FAITH, <u>stirred up</u>.** If you intend on drinking from the pot of success again, dust yourself off and try again. You've got to believe that you can. Note, a jug, a measure of increased capacity, is required where faith is required.

For this next ingredient you will have to put a strainer or a sieve over the pot to ensure that you **<u>recognise and catch it</u>**, the right one… Its **OPPORTUNITY**. Once you have recognised the opportunity, you have to respond to it with **<u>COURAGE</u>**, another key ingredient for this pot of success.

A dash of willingness will complement opportunity nicely. Notice we are adding a dash. Be willing to the point of doing what is required of you, without being sucked in and sent off your path. Stand close enough to the goal to access it, yet far enough back to still see with clarity.

THE SECRET INGREDIENT: <u>BE YOU</u>. Add your character, your nature, the fact that you are the first and the best as you are, that you are enough as you are. That you are made for this goal. The goal responds to you. Walking in your own unique purpose and being yourself, even if you've changed a bit now, that will make this time around better, the pot of success will overflow, you will have dusted yourself off, tried again AND SUCCEEDED!

THE CONCEPT OF TRYING AGAIN

Wisdom tells you not to fall victim to the things you once did, and so you really have to weigh up if something that you want to revisit is worth it and is the most practical route to take for you. With that being said, I feel that there is somewhat of a stigma around re visiting something that you had previously let go of. A stigma that doesn't take account of all the different factors or reasons for why you let go in the first place. If you know that you are not satisfied with the way something was left and you feel that you have the tools and the capacity to pick it back up and run with the vision; do so. Do not delay.

I get it, you fell off, it didn't feel good. You have a second, third or maybe even fourth chance at it now. Dust yourself off by commanding the thoughts in the territory of your mind to be subject to the things that will lead to your goals; things like focus, determination, and consistency.

In closing, **WOMAN**, as you dust yourself and prepare to try again, I urge you to consider;

Associations, watch who you walk with: Can two walk together unless they be in agreement? (Amos 3:3)

Lessons learned from previous disappointments, how you will use them going forward?: Be committed to ALWAYS asking the questions; What can I learn from this and where will the paving stones of this lesson lead me? **A contingency; that it is not a sign of surrender, but of wisdom:** What happens when…? What happens if…?

Forgiveness: Release others AND yourself.

Your belief system: Let go of fear, switch out doubt for FAITH

YOU: Consider yourself, that you are made for whatever you are chasing that is in alignment with your purpose.

May you be richly blessed as you take steps to dust yourself off and try again; as you move into your purpose and your destiny.

Remembering always,
that YOU ARE THE FIRST AND THE BEST

Tales of Womanhood Vol 2

TARA BURGIN

Tara Burgin tells her story of how she struggled to survive and create a better future for herself and her daughter. This was her ultimate driving force.

After falling pregnant at the age of 19 she describes herself as feeling lost, confused and empty. The doctors later confirmed that she was suffering from post-natal depression.

Later she realised that she was not a product of her failures rather a work in progress and the pain and struggle was only defining and strengthening her character to propel her to the next chapter in her life.

At the age of 27 Tara opened her own children's day nursery. Tara believes that in life we must endure the struggle and see every set back and every negative word spoken as an opportunity to propel us, so we are able to progress on to the next stage in our life or business.

She is now a strong advocate for empowering others through her work as a Business and Empowerment Coach and Speaker. Tara uses her 10 years of business expertise, lessons and failures to empower entrepreneurs.

CHAPTER 7
THE BIRTH OF AN ENTREPRENEUR
TARA BURGIN

"It is better to stand alone than with people who do not value you."

My Childhood

My dollies were lined up neatly against the wall of my double bedroom, which once used to be my brothers' room which they had shared. I am the third child.

My notebook in one hand and my pen in the other I call each dollies name; peering over my book waiting patiently as though one of the dollies were really going to respond. My mum always said I would grow up to be either a teacher or someone who would work with children in one way or another.

I remember my dad describing me as always being a shy introverted child growing up. I feared going to the shop or walking to school and did these things way beyond the expected milestone age. If there was ever a question asked, I would be the girl at the back of the class not being noticed. I was non-expressive and was the opposite of my second youngest brother.

Home life was quite secluded and strict. I partially grew up in the times where both my parents had believed children should be seen and not heard. Mum often re-told the stories of how I took a long time to read and write, she remembers the many times she would sit with me at night with my books.

Mum had worked hard to get away from the nursing

career she once had; those were the dreaded times I used to sit in the house of an elderly lady and watch whilst my mum changed the bed pan. It wasn't the best of way for a young child to spend their time but it made ends meet. Upon reflection it was no wonder that when mum finally was teaching in a local special needs school that both my parents were so stringent about education. Even up until this day I can hear my mother's voice echoing G.C.S.E's, G.C.S.E's that's all you'll ever need to win at life. Literally nothing else seemed to matter to them, however, to their disappointment I wasn't the A student that they had hoped me to be.

The Struggle

After my year in college and qualifying as a Nursery Nurse I found myself a job in a local day nursery I thoroughly enjoyed my job and was happy in my role, but at this stage I'd never truly really found myself, I didn't know my core values or who I stood for as a person, I guess you could say I never really connected with my inner self. I know this now looking back on some of my failed relationships. I would always crumble every time things went wrong; how could people have an effect on me like this. I realise now that I was insecure and needed that validation from someone to make me feel happy and worthy. I searched for a long time seeking happiness in others however...

...Happiness is an inside job we shouldn't look for it in others or seek validation from others but only seek this in ourselves.

Fast forward on & I fell pregnant with my daughter. I was happy and well during my pregnancy but when my daughter was born, my feelings changed. I felt like I was slowly suffocating. It felt like my world had now caved in on me. Feelings of confusion and overwhelm totally consumed me. I questioned myself and my ability to care for this small tiny baby weighing in a mere 6lbs 11 ounces. I remember the time when the nurse came to my bed and was trying to wake me up saying, 'your baby is crying.' I could hear the voice of the nurse faintly and then it became louder as she towered over my bed, was I dreaming or was this real? I was just a baby myself at the tender age of 19. Was this really happening to me?

Being in a strange environment, surrounded by nurses and other mothers who all seemed to know what they were doing with their new-borns, I was the youngest mother on the ward which made me feel insignificant and different. The strong strange smell of the hospital powerfully reminding me that this was as real as ever.

I tried to look on the bright side. Mum said things would get better once I came home, I couldn't wait for that day. It was probably the slowest time ever. Seven days has never felt so long in my entire life. It didn't help that Xmas was in just a few days. A time when I should've been at home with my family around, with mum and dad, and opening my pressies, this made me even more miserable and depressed.

Complications during and after the birth meant that I had to stay in longer than anticipated. I was given a drip which went right through me and collected my urine. I held this delicately when I dared to use the toilet. The thought of the toilet haunted me. I can still remember the burning, stinging sensation as I peed. It had become so painful that I was no longer passing urine.

Finally, I was home and things appeared normal. The warmly homely feel and the smell of mum's cooking had never felt so good. Shaniah was wrapped in a blanket and laid in her rocker with not a care to the world. Her sweet cute innocence beamed all around her.

After the holidays mum went back to work. Shaniah's dad was staying with me and this was comforting, however when everyone left the house for work in the morning, it was extremely lonely, and dark loomed all around. The isolation and coldness surrounded me. There was no one to talk too, no one to express how I was feeling to, no help with caring for my baby.

I tried to leave the house at times just to get out and about, but this took me forever to do and I was always so tired. When I eventually decided to take a stroll it felt as though everyone was staring at me, judging me for having my baby at such a young age.

One day a family friend approached me in the street and said,

"Why did you do that"

"Why did I do what" I replied

"Why did you have the baby? You know you've made this very hard on yourself?"

If my face were a glass you would have seen all the pieces shattering into small tiny bits, this broke me entirely & left me speechless and shocked. From that day I don't remember venturing out much at all unless I was with mum or dad.

Shine Bright

I often felt lost and worthless, destined to a life of emptiness. My day to day felt like a chore and that blissful feeling of joy and happiness that most mothers speak of sadly I never felt.

The doctor prescribed me with anti-depressants, and I was suffering from post-natal depression. At home I felt trapped all day and night and I just knew I had to escape this life.

By the time my daughter was three months I went back to work. The frustration and loneliness drove me back to employment. It was then I started to reflect on my life and where I was really going with my future. I didn't realise how dire my situation was until I could no longer get the things I once could afford. Then there was the mental and emotional strain of caring for my daughter and working with more children at work. It was driving me mad I thought I was in a day care morning noon and night. What once was a career that I had admired made me gloomy and I started to think about the life I wanted to create for myself, but it was much deeper than that, what life would I create for my daughter who solely depended on me?

I knew if things were going to get better I had to re-build myself in order for me and my daughter to have a better future. My mindset was the first thing that needed to change I had to see my situation for what it was and return to studies to better myself, the determination set in.

I had a clear purpose and I was on a mission, the next few years saw me go back to study, and I graduated from Uni with a 2:1 in Early Years Education with I.T

I applied for every job going. There were knock backs but every set back began to make me more determined to succeed. My mindset had upgraded, it was stronger than ever and I was more destined towards reaching my goal. I went on to seek higher positions which meant no longer being just the nursery assistant. After a struggle I eventually found a job as Deputy Manager. I was totally ecstatic, hard work was finally paying off. The pay was good for that time and I thoroughly enjoyed my job, however the post didn't last long and I found myself back at square one. I took a bit of time out to reflect on my current state and where I was. I had a choice either I could continue this life hustling, or I could rise to another level, a higher version of myself. I knew I had more to give. I had become very ambitious, I felt even more determined to strive for a better future.

I am not defined by my failures or past challenges rather I am a work in progress of it and either I use the lessons to strengthen and propel me to the next level in my life or I allow it to hold me in bondage.

It was at this very moment that my epiphany struck me, could this be the breakthrough that I was really destined for.
"I know what I'll do mum, I said I 'll open my own day nursery'
Mum looked at me and said "Yes you can do that"
That was all I needed to hear and at that moment I began

to visualise the day nursery. I pictured happy parents and families dropping off their children. The kids excited to enter their nursery dressed in a uniform; they looked so cute. I wasn't just a Manager but the Owner Director, my face beamed with excitement. I remember telling a few people about my idea, the vision very clear in my mind, but most people doubtfully questioned me with a few people even saying it was a crazy idea and it probably wouldn't work. This slightly dampened my spirit, but this did not put me off rather this made me even more determined to set up.

From my struggles I realised the strength and determination I had built up was just the strength I needed to open this day nursery and take on this immense idea.

The struggle will not give you anything that you cannot cope with, for as long as you do not quit.

I was ready to take on this exciting yet very challenging and somewhat frightening endeavour.

The Blessing in Disguise

In 2009 my dream became a reality and I opened my very own Day Nursery. The nursery was set-in well-maintained premises with an adjacent park and outdoor area to the rear of the building. T nursery would hold a maximum of 50 children aged 1 – 5 years of age. Inside it comprised three rooms, the main large room the office and the kitchen area. It was all very surreal but so exciting, a blend of feelings and emotions including euphoria. The nursery was a true reflection of what I expected of my very own setting, this included a range of extra- curricular activities from French to Dance and Drama. The setting offered a home reading club for the pre-school aged children and both parent and child would select a book together. The children wore uniform, which looked so cute just like I had imagined. To be honest I couldn't have done all this without the support from mum.

We had a glossy brochure which reflected the setting inside and out. Two images of children were on the front cover, which included my daughter Shaniah:- my main driving force for starting the project and who had brought me to this amazing point in my journey. My daughter was really a blessing in disguise. All the struggles I had previously endured seemed so worth it as without her I would have never ventured towards this idea.

On Reflection

Throughout parts of my journey I have needed to reflect on my life and see my situation for what it was. Your failures or past mistakes do not define who you are, they are just work in progress of what is yet to come, providing you learn from the mistakes and do not quit. Sometimes it can be hard to reflect especially if you are caught up with emotions or self-pity. Try to seek the driving force in your situation. In my case my daughter was my drive and the desperation for wanting to have a better future.

People will talk about you and form their own judgement. Learn to love yourself more than their opinions and allow your purpose to drive you to your full potential. Remember that hardship is temporary and is needed to harden us at times to bring a better package of you to the next stage of your life.

From my struggles, I'm now passionate about helping others to move forward & to help them realise their worth and overcome their challenges in their life or business

Tales of Womanhood Vol 2

Tales of Womanhood Vol 2

TSITSI CHIPENDO

'My health Journal' is an extract from Tsitsi's second book, 'Finding Him in the Mystery.' Born and raised in a Christian family, Tsitsi has developed her trust and ability to find God in the mysteries of life, one of which she talks about in this book, Tales of Womanhood. She writes about a health challenge she experienced soon after relocating to Australia in 2014 with symptoms consistent with neurological deficits although scans detected nil abnormalities.

Her first book is called Understanding Prophecy. In that book she reveals that every word that prophets in the Old Testament uttered, got fulfilled in Jesus, making it safer for the modern day Christian to believe in prophecy. Tsitsi wears a 'coat of many colours' for real. She is not only a writer but also a singer and a composer. Together with her twin Rudo, she has recorded two albums.

She holds various accounting qualifications, including the Institute of Chartered Secretaries and Administrators in Zimbabwe (ICSAZ). Tsitsi is now living in Australia and working as an Enrolled Nurse. She is due to graduate with a Bachelor of Registered Nursing in October, 2019.

CHAPTER 8
MY HEALTH JOURNAL
TSITSI CHIPENDO

"Whatever is happening to you, your spirit is above it."

My health journal 1

The excitement of leaving my native country to go to Australia was shortly reversed by a series of events ranging from weather conditions to things that I myself could not even categorise. Thoughts of doubt, impossibilities and defeat found habitation in my little mind, making it impossible to believe that I would ever make it. Every reason to rejoice had been reversed. As each day passed, hopelessness was getting stronger and stronger. I wondered, 'Am I dreaming, is this surely happening, why, for how long...?' This period seemed like an eternity. My life had taken a different turn and my future looked bleak. Going back home was not an option, given my circumstances.

With no one to talk to, no words to express the feeling, pain and symptoms, the only road I could see was the road to nowhere. I didn't know what to call it, but it was certainly not life. To regard all that was happening as normal was painful. People around me seemed to be enjoying life, achieving their daily goals and even planning for the next day. This issue was eating me up. It felt as if an invincible power had surrounded me.

Being in a strange land with no family, my chances of making it were diminishing by the day. Fear had taken its toll on me and pride too was haunting me down. 'Should I tell them?' This daily debate in my head was not only confusing but also left me feeling guilty. Desperation was the only force that would persuade me to search for help, but another part of me did not want to take any more risks. 'What will they think about me?' I didn't want to be let down again. Though I could feel something had gone terribly wrong, I was not prepared to let anyone know.

I had planned to find my own place as soon as I got a job. I strengthened myself and braced myself for the unknown. The South African girl I had met in the city had come at the right time. Her role was to link me with Ali, a lady who owned a cleaning company who was soon to hire me. That saw me moving out towards the northern suburbs, more than 50km away from where I was.

Before taking up the job offer with Ali, my previous attempts had seen me visiting the Catholic church looking for help. Two issues were pertinent then. I needed help with school fees and accommodation. The church was willing to help me get allowances from the government but as soon as they learnt that I was on a student visa, they aborted the process.

I approached my school for help in the form of a scholarships and was told they did not have any packages for international students. I asked if I could let immigration know of my predicament and thank goodness, the student adviser was kind enough to indicate that was not a good option as that would get my visa cancelled.

The church later linked me with an Indian family that was willing to help me with accommodation in return for helping with household chores and school runs for their children. The only challenge was my health. Whatever it was, it was getting aggressive by the day, a mystery that I did not want anyone to know. So, I took the cleaning option, that way I would gain independence and control.

I had not completely moved out of my current residence. I was still working on the logistics. I remember one particular morning, it was before 0500hrs when I was going to the bus station. It was freezing cold, dead silent and no car could be seen or heard in the vicinity. Then, all of a sudden hell broke loose on me. From having shivering episodes to feeling extremely hot as if fire was burning in my body. I took off my jacket and walking became an uphill task. I could hardly move my legs. I experienced difficulty in lifting them as if there was a force opposing my movement. The road had a bit of gradient and was moving up, each attempt would be thwarted by running out of breath. I decided to stop and make a short prayer. I said, 'God let there be a car that I am going to wave at, and that car will stop and take me to the bus station'.

The Lord was faithful, in less than 10 minutes a car appeared that was going in the same direction as me. To my surprise two Africans were in the car. They said to me, ' you must be a Christian, we don't stop for anyone.'

How true it was. They asked why I did not have any warm clothes. They were shocked when I told them I was feeling hot. As we talked, we realised that we were from the same country but from different provinces. They were from Matebeleland and I was from Mashonaland. I was grateful for their help. They took me to the train station. I had made it a point that I would not disclose my predicament to anyone.

At this time, I was not sure if I would survive one more day. I had lots of questions. I was so heartbroken, became desperate and afraid of seeing my life fade away right in front of me. Guilt, resentment, grief, pain, worry and regret flooded my mind at the same time. I could not remember a time when I had enjoyed good health. My childhood was characterised by various kinds of illnesses. Most of them were considered normal. Yes, catching a cold, tonsillitis and stuff like that is common in children, but in my case, it was over the top.

I remember a time when doctors decided to have my tonsils removed. My parents were hesitant. They feared they would lose me. At first, they said no. But because this was recurring at short intervals, they had no choice but to follow the doctor's advice. Each time they took me for the procedure, something would happen. On one occasion I had something to eat before going to the hospital, so they had to cancel the operation. On three separate occasions, for some reason my name could not be found on the list. My parents gave up, hoping that one day the problem would go on its own.

My health journal 2

I can't really talk about my life without mentioning that I have a twin sibling. Health wise my sister was thriving. I was feeble and really struggling. I had chest pains and would be affected by winter temperatures. Because my mother was working in a hospital, she appreciated health matters a bit more than others in the family. Whenever I fell sick my mother would take me for check- ups. What my family found difficult to understand was the failure by doctors to diagnose my problems. It was one health challenge after the other. On a bad day my school bag would be heavy, and my twin sister would have to come to my rescue.

The third eldest in our family thought I was making up stories to cover up for my laziness. I was not the kind of person that would help with house work though. I always had excuses. At times I would bluntly refuse. But one of the reasons was that whenever I tried to clean the floor and use a bit of strength, I would run out of breath, so that was difficult. As I got older, I realised that as childhood problems got phased out, newer challenges were developing.

My family were giving me all the support I needed, and my father was hard on all of us with regards to school work. He would say to us (twins) that if we failed in school, we would be married to some village men that would make us adopt a village lifestyle. The sound of it was so depressing to the ears. Each time he spoke like that, we promised to surprise him. To that, our father would say, 'you better do…' I believed what my father had said and was convinced that I had no option but to study really hard if I did not want to experience more problems later in life. I did my best, studied accounting, went for higher qualifications and achieved one of my goals which was relocating to Australia. Little did I know that the mystery was yet to unfold.

Uncertainty was now a part of me. Each day never gave me a reason to believe I would see the next one. It was now seven years since our mum had died, the only one who had been there for me. She did not really need anyone to tell her if I was unwell. Whenever she suspected I had an infection she would treat me using home- made therapies. Though I did not like her interventions that much, they worked. Sometimes after arriving home from work she would have to go back, but this time with me because something would be wrong. I remember I was unwell when she died, and my twin sister encouraged me to be strong because no one was going to be available for me as our mum had been. How true it was.

I remember the times she would cover me with additional blankets in winter. I could not stand the cold. I recall a time when my sister and I had gotten an opportunity to relocate to England. Our father was quite opposed to the idea because of my health. He feared I would not cope with the cold. What I found frustrating was seeking medical help and not being able to get it. My life was filled with deep sadness and hopelessness as a result. My parents were desperate too and did what any other parent would do in such circumstances, they tried alternative therapies as well as traditional methods, but all that was in vain.

My health journal 3

I had just returned from a long-day's cleaning job, feeling exhausted. I had kept the early morning experience to myself. I was going to spend the night at Mireune's place, the girl from church that visited me after learning that a new member had arrived from Africa, she was lovely. She had prepared her best meal for me, but I did not have much of an appetite and strength to eat. She offered me a packet of salt and vinegar crisps and I decided to have some. In no time, I felt as if all the water in my body had been sucked out, I experienced an excessive thirst that threatened my life.

I was not sure if I still had any time left on this earth. There was a spiral of events from then on. Thoughts of regret overshadowed my mind. I wondered why I had not thought of letting my family know that I had been confronted by a strong giant. Immediately my whole life appeared right before me, I could see everything from when I was a child to where I had reached. By now I was convinced that death was inevitable. I could not utter that term before, although its process had begun. I became weak and stiff at the same time in one side of my body. Severe cramps and a numbing sensation spread all over my body. As whispers of past failures by doctors to help me got louder in my ear I decided not to let Mireune know. I was ashamed of myself too, I had never heard of anyone with similar symptoms. My pride gave me strong reasons to keep this struggle to myself. I remember one doctor saying to my mum, 'though your daughter is not looking well, we are limited as to what we can do as we lack an objective basis on which to rest our decisions.' Since then, I didn't believe anyone was able to help me.

My life in Australia was characterised by weird crippling pains. My whole body would go numb, what kind of disease was it? Who was going to give me answers? What a mystery, no one had any idea that something was weighing me down. Some people thought I had made it in life, little did they know life itself had locked me in a world of my own.

As the pain increased, I decided to swallow my pride and let my family know what was going on. I was hesitant at first, I feared my father would not be able to handle the news. You know, there comes a time when you do not want your parent to know your troubles. You weigh up the risk, and when you realise that they may get even more troubled you try and solve your problems silently. I decided to break the news and thought, '...he will come to terms with my death'.

I thought of my twin sister, Rudo. I could imagine the pain and impact that would have on her. Being twins has never been easy. You can't separate twins. Life had been difficult when all my efforts to be close to my sister failed. God helped me understand that though we were twins he had separate plans for each one of us.

My health journal 4

My sister and I had wanted to study law soon after high school, but because we did not have the required points to be considered for the programme we did not get admission into university. That saw my sister embarking on her second best course in accounting studies, the Chartered Institute of Secretaries (CIS). I perceived accounting to be challenging, so I suggested that we do a six month secretarial course instead. My sister did not see that as an option. She was the kind of person who would say, 'I don't want to be somebody's secretary. I would rather have a secretary of my own'. The same accounting programme was going to let her realise her dreams. Though I doubted I would make it in the accounting field, I still followed her as I wanted to maintain the 'identical' part of the twins equation.

On the other hand, I had had nursing at the back of my mind since my childhood days. I asked my sister to join me in submitting applications for the same but she was reluctant, she had her mind made up, she told me nursing was not an option for her. So, do you want to guess what I did? I started submitting applications for the two of us. To my greatest surprise they called my sister and not me. I was happy and jealous at the same time. I wondered why they did not call me. 'Yes its ok to have called her, but how about me?' My twin did not even want to go for the interview. She later agreed to attend the interview after family members had a serious talk with her. When she returned from the interview she was so happy that they had offered her a place to train as a nurse.

My mother tried to help me get in as well but that was to no avail. That is when we first separated. What a painful experience it was. On the other hand, I kept on doing my accounting studies and God helping I achieved great heights in that field. My sister had to leave her accounting studies and focus on nursing and she too made good progress in her field. My sister got married, that was another blow. It was difficult to handle this seemingly permanent separation. Against all odds, I went and stayed with her. Surely everyone must understand, you shouldn't separate twins.

One of the sisters in church said something I found profound and which has been enshrined in my heart ever since. She said in moments like this when you miss your twin, ask the Holy Spirit to take her place. I found it true because God was about to make it clear to us that though we were twins he wanted each one of us to rely on him.

Another aspect about us, is that we operate at more or less the same wave length. If my sister tells me she is not ok, I sort of know what she means and vice versa. The struggle continued, and I wondered 'how do I let her know?' I was not sure how she would react to the news I was about to break. She had an idea from before that my health was not that intact. But she had no idea about this level of my poor health. A slight hint would send her into deep thoughts. It would be the same for me, if she was in a similar situation. I regretted the idea of leaving Zimbabwe. 'Did I really have to go abroad to die? What are people going to say?' I was now in my third month in Australia.

My health journal 5

After I had thought long and hard about it, I thought, 'she too will have to be ok when I'm gone.' I sent her this message, 'whole body cramping'.

A new debate started in my mind. I recalled a time when my twin's second baby had a fever. My sister panicked and took the baby to the emergency rooms crying. The following day the baby was fine. When my sister narrated this to another sister, Eurita in church she laughed and said, 'my sister when you cry the devil laughs....'

She said crying signifies defeat. In no time, inner strength started welling up in my spirit and I started fighting back.

It felt as if my whole body had frozen, my right side got cold instantly. When I realised I still had a bit of movement in my left side, I decided to do all that my hands would allow me to do. I did not have enough strength to write long messages. For a long time, my pride had prevented me from seeking help, but now I was in excruciating pain and I needed help. I finally let Mireune know. I asked her to call our pastor Tony, who happened to be based in a different state, Melbourne. I recall what he said, **'whatever is happening to you, your spirit is above it'**.

He prayed for me over the phone and asked Mireune to call for an ambulance. I could not care less, whichever way,

I was going to die. We waited for the paramedics to come.

My family now had an idea that I was unwell. I had sent a message on our family WhatsApp group platform saying, 'please pray for me.'

The eldest in my family did not waste time, she called to find out what was happening. I started crying as I narrated my pain. She started praying, 'Oh Lord you know what has gone wrong in my sister's body, please fix it.' After prayer she made a guess, she said she thought I had a severe electrolyte imbalance. She promised me I would be ok. Realising I would be going to hospital, she stayed on the line and got the chance to speak with the paramedics. Communication was a barrier, my spoken English was not that good, so she told them everything I had said to her. Mirene was with me, she went with me to the hospital. The symptoms mimicked stroke or heart attack, they treated me to prevent further deterioration.

This all happened in August, the same month my mother had died. I thought I was not meant to live beyond the month of August, but the devil has been a liar all his life. God always arises and our enemies are destroyed. I recall as the month started, I had received some prayer points from our chapter from back home. August had been declared a month of fasting and praying against sickness and diseases. We were instructed to break the holy communion as we prayed. For the first two days I did not pray, and later I asked myself why I had not taken the call to pray seriously as my own health had started deteriorating. I joined in the prayers and followed the programme. We had prayer points to use. I would pray in the morning and evening. I remember watching a sermon by pastor Chris called the Impact of the Holy Spirit on the Human body. I can't recall for how many times I listened to that sermon. It was as if he was saying to me, your body needs the touch of God. How true it was.

My health journal 6

I remember when we were towards the last two weeks of August my prayer had changed. I did not have any more words, I would start crying. I would go on and on, not knowing why I was sensing the need for more of God. When I was able to speak, I would ask God and say, 'Is there a time I planned to worship a different God that is not you... do you know that I love you?' Why it was happening only God knows.

The paramedics had instructed my friend not to give me any food or water. By now it was clear that death was an inch away. But I now needed God to help me. Some of the things that were prolonging my departure were the people I did not want to let down.

That journey will be painful when you have excess baggage. Mine was my family, my father and my twin mainly. I said of all people, not my twin. But as I released each one of them it was soon to happen. But there kept on coming unresolved issues. I am a singer, writer and had so many tasks that were still on my to do list. It became apparent that I had not fulfilled my purpose. That one was even worse.

I asked God to help me with advice, I said to Him, 'I know you will ask me about this, how am I going to answer you.' You know what the bible says is true. There are things that you may ignore or argue with now, but when that time comes it will be clear that God's purpose is the only reason we live. That part was even difficult.

Before, I had lots of questions. I wondered why God had let the mystery surrounding my health remain hidden. It appeared as if God had been over powered by the devil himself. Yes, the same problem that troubled me from my childhood was about to win the trophy over my life and God seemed to have distanced Himself from me. Who then could deliver me from that powerful enemy?

I did not want to think about it again. I simply had to accept the position and be grateful otherwise the process would be prolonged again, so unbearable leaving you with no other option but to come to terms with everything, both finished and unfinished business. It's amazing, in those few minutes I had lots of conversations started and finished. Another part of me was getting ready to check out of this world while another one was saying, 'but you can fight back…'

So, my twin's story about her baby Hannah, rang in mind and the response from the sister at church and I said, 'no, devil you are lying. I am not dying'. I said, 'God if you say its ok, I will go but if it's because of the wicked one no, I will fight.' I started praying under my voice all the way to the hospital. My prayer was 'Christ is the one living in me, not me. His faith not mine. I was saying God if you can't see my faith, see Jesus' faith.' I remembered what our pastor had taught in the sermon I watched. He said to pray in tongues, so I did that as well, I said if it works it will work for me, if it doesn't then we will see.

You know in the emergency department, there are emergency cases that need to be dealt with urgently. No doctor came to see me until about four hours later. The symptoms had gotten better, and I said, 'God, this is what I mean, no one will believe me if I told them I could not move, they will not see anything wrong in me. That is why I did not want to come to the hospital.' Later on, one of the doctors attended to me and upon finishing narrating my story, his immediate reaction was 'strange'. At that I took offence, 'comments like this make it difficult for me to open up'. I told God.

My health journal 7

My sister was calling and speaking with the doctors, these doctors were accommodating, they let my sister make suggestions. I had bloods done and the results were too shocking to be true. The results were incompatible with life, the doctor told me later. He said to me, 'now I know why you are having all this. YOU HAVE NO BLOOD! It's almost zero.' The nurses did not waste time, instantly my room was flooded with these wonderful people wanting to save my life. They said to me my body was shutting down and if I had not come to the hospital it was not going to be good news for my family.

The lovely team resuscitated me with various blood products and for the first time in a long while I felt strength building up in me. Of particular interest was my eyes. They were red when I woke up, something I had never seen before. I used to think my twin sister had a problem when her eyes would turn red even after a short nap. That same morning I was seen by a team of doctors that had come to gather more information about my medical history. They expressed shock, disbelief and compassion at the same time. They explained my blood circulation had been compromised and my body had started shutting down. 'It doesn't happen, it has never happened...' they exclaimed. Everyone in my family was speechless. 'Oh no Tsitsi... what has been happening to you...?' At last the mystery was getting clearer and clearer. But was it the one that was haunting my life all along? Another chapter had started, yes, a new lease of life granted, but was it all...? Doctors told me they were determined to understand why I had such a low blood count. To be continued......

My advice

Many believers are of the view that Christianity is the end of problems, but the bible does make it clear that many hardships and perplexing situations do confront believers. Being a Christian does not mean the absence of problems, it is about how you overcome them. Even after David had been anointed by Samuel to be King of Israel we see him going through many problems in his life, to the extent that the then King who also happened to be his father in law, Saul, tried on several occasions to kill him, but because of faith, trust and patience in God, he overcame it all and became a great, prosperous and peaceful king.

To anyone that might be facing any form of difficulty, just know that your situation will not have defeat as its final result. It will become an occasion to show God's glory.

Tales of Womanhood Vol 2

Tales of Womanhood Vol 2

ABOUT THE COMPLILER
MAUREEN MBONDIAH-MANDIPAZA

"When the storm comes for an eagle it is time to excel to greater heights"

Hello my name is Maureen Mbondiah-Mandipaza. I am a multi award winning entrepreneur with a successful healthcare business and various other businesses that I have built up from scratch.

Unapologetically I am a successful Woman in Business, Philanthropist, A Speaker and an Author.

I am passionate about inspiring women in business and recently started my own mentoring business called MoMentors.

I have won many awards including Be Mogul and Woman to Watch.

Apart from helping women in business through my mentorship programmes, I also inspire women through writing.

My Anthology book project Tales of Womanhood is a platform I started in 2018 to allow women from all walks of life to share their life challenges by contributing a chapter to the book series.

The book series has been simply designed to encourage you with inspirational real life stories of women just like me and you, who have also passed through difficulties and made it to the finish line.

My desire is to inspired you to be More and to do More hence MoMentors

The Good News is you too can share your story in the next book.

My Achievements to date

- All Women Achievers Awards 2016 Finalist
- Midlands Business and Community Awards 2016
- BEFTA Awards 2016
- Breakfree Recognition Award 2015
- Women of Purpose Recognition Award 2016
- Divas of Colour Nominee 2017
- International Runway Achievers Award Nominee 2017
- Powerhouse Global Awards 2017 for Service Provider Awards "Winner"
- MBCC Awards 2017 "Carer of the Year Award" Finalwsist "
- NOWA Awards 2017 Woman in Business "Winner"
- EAWA "Philanthropist of the year "2017 Nominee
- Women 4 Africa 2018 Nominee Finalist Women in Healthcare
- Women of the World 2018 Nominee
. Be Mogul Award Winner 2018/2019
. Be Mogul Woman to Watch Winner 2018/2019

Tales of Womanhood Vol 2

Tales of Womanhood Vol 2

SUSAN BROOKES -MORRIS

Susan is the founder of Positive Publicity which offers copywriting, editing and publicity services. She loves promoting positive stories and sharing the good work of others.

She has contributed to three books:- The Book of Soulful Musings, Inspiring Conversations to live Life with Love, Intention, Flow, Ease (Chrisoula Sirigou), Believe You Can Face Your Fears and Confidently Claim the Life You Desire(Sue Williams), Embracing & Releasing the Celebrity in You, Inspiring Stories for Women in Business (I AM Woman).

Susan also runs Positive Kids which organises events, produces a magazine and has a Facebook discussion forum. These services are designed to help us all raise healthy and happy kids who have great self-esteem, confidence, resilience and know how to be physically healthy and safe.

Susan lives near Birmingham in England with her family.

EDITOR'S COMMENTS

'Be The Driver In Your Life, Not The Passenger.'

It has been so inspiring to read and edit these very personal stories within this fabulous book. All the contributors have faced many adversities including abuse, low self-esteem, discrimination, intimidation and health issues, yet all have risen to be successful in their own right and have a greater awareness and understanding of themselves and others.

I praise their generosity and authenticity in sharing their stories. I know that readers will gain strength and encouragement to deal with their own challenges and lead the best lives they can through reading these tales.

I have certainly gained much from reading the stories of others. I agree with all the co-authors that with strength and tenacity we can all be the best version of ourselves. That does not mean however that we should not seek help and support from others and challenge unfairness and discrimination.

I wish all readers well and encourage you to lead your own life with positivity and purpose. As my chapter in the Believe You Can book says, 'Be the driver in your life, not the passenger,' remember you do not have to stay stuck and be unhappy, you can choose to make changes. If you are already leading a contented life, you have the ability to do even more, just believe in yourself, take every opportunity to learn and develop and take positive and consistent action.

By Susan Brookes-Morris

PAGES FOR YOUR NOTES

Tales of Womanhood Vol 2

PAGES FOR YOUR NOTES

HAVE YOU READ TALES OF WOMANHOOD VOLUME 1 YET?

AVAILABLE TO BUY ON AMAZON

If you would like you would like to be part of Volume 3. Contact Maureen Mbondiah-Mandipaza at: womanhoodglobal@gmail.com
www.talesofwomanhood.org

Tales of Womanhood Vol 2